# 500 Recipes and Hints for Freezing

# 500 RECIPES AND HINTS FOR FREEZING

by Audrey Ellis

HAMLYN

Published by Hamlyn Publishing,
a division of The Hamlyn Publishing Group Limited,
Bridge House, London Road, Twickenham,
Middlesex, England

Seventh impression 1985

ISBN 0 600 33631 X

Printed and bound in Great Britain by
R. J. Acford

# Contents

# Introduction

The freezer is now a valued piece of domestic equipment in so many homes that people are beginning to cook in an entirely new way. No longer does a housewife decide to make a batch of scones for tea and perhaps a few extra to keep until the next day. Today she is far more likely to decide that this would be a good time to make scones, so she mixes sufficient dough to bake off fruit scones for tea, one tray with cheese instead of fruit for supper later in the week, and another tray with chopped fresh herbs as well for a future picnic treat. A little planning along these lines goes a long way to help you get the best from your freezer.

The old-fashioned idea that the home maker must be a slave to her household tasks has given way to a totally new approach. The freezer, like the washing machine in its time, has introduced a totally new concept: that chores can be done in the most labour-saving way and at the times which suit you best. Even if you make no elaborate plans to keep the freezer stocked, but cook a double quantity or bake two cakes instead of one whenever the impulse seizes you, the stocks tend to take care of themselves. You will always have some ready-cooked dishes to draw on. Nevertheless, the planning and carrying out of occasional big cook-ins is something in the nature of a hobby with many happy freezer owners.

This book provides a huge choice of simple and straight-forward recipes all of which are happy to find a temporary home in the freezer.

*Audrey Ellis*

# Useful Facts and Figures

## Notes on metrication

In this book quantities are given in metric and Imperial measures. Exact conversion from Imperial to metric measures does not usually give very convenient working quantities and so the metric measures have been rounded off into units of 25 grams. The table below shows the recommended equivalents.

| Ounces | Approx g to nearest whole figure | Recommended conversion to nearest unit of 25 |
|---|---|---|
| 1 | 28 | 25 |
| 2 | 57 | 50 |
| 3 | 85 | 75 |
| 4 | 113 | 100 |
| 5 | 142 | 150 |
| 6 | 170 | 175 |
| 7 | 198 | 200 |
| 8 | 227 | 225 |
| 9 | 255 | 250 |
| 10 | 283 | 275 |
| 11 | 312 | 300 |
| 12 | 340 | 350 |
| 13 | 368 | 375 |
| 14 | 396 | 400 |
| 15 | 425 | 425 |
| 16 (1 lb) | 454 | 450 |
| 17 | 482 | 475 |
| 18 | 510 | 500 |
| 19 | 539 | 550 |
| 20 (1¼ lb) | 567 | 575 |

**Note:**
When converting quantities over 20 oz first add the appropriate figures in the centre column, then adjust to the nearest unit of 25. As a general guide, 1 kg (1000 g) equals 2·2 lb or about 2 lb 3 oz. This method of conversion gives good results in nearly all cases, although in certain pastry and cake recipes a more accurate conversion is necessary to produce a balanced recipe.

**Liquid measures:** The millilitre has been used in this book and the following table gives a few examples.

| Imperial | Approx ml to nearest whole figure | Recommended ml |
|---|---|---|
| ¼ pint | 142 | 150 ml |
| ½ pint | 283 | 300 ml |
| ¾ pint | 425 | 450 ml |
| 1 pint | 567 | 600 ml |
| 1½ pints | 851 | 900 ml |
| 1¾ pints | 992 | 1000 ml (1 litre) |

**Spoon measures:** All spoon measures given in this book are level unless otherwise stated.

**Can sizes:** At present, cans are marked with the exact (usually to the nearest whole number) metric equivalent of the Imperial weight of the contents, so we have followed this practice when giving can sizes.

# Oven temperatures

The table below gives recommended equivalents.

|  | °F | °C | Gas Mark |
|---|---|---|---|
| Very cool | 110 | 225 | $\frac{1}{4}$ |
|  | 120 | 250 | $\frac{1}{2}$ |
| Cool | 140 | 275 | 1 |
|  | 150 | 300 | 2 |
| Moderate | 160 | 325 | 3 |
|  | 180 | 350 | 4 |
| Moderately hot | 190 | 375 | 5 |
|  | 200 | 400 | 6 |
| Hot | 220 | 425 | 7 |
|  | 230 | 450 | 8 |
| Very hot | 240 | 475 | 9 |

# Notes for American and Australian users

In America the 8-oz measuring cup is used. In Australia metric measures are now used in conjunction with the standard 250-ml measuring cup. The Imperial pint, used in Britain and Australia, is 20 fl oz, while the American pint is 16 fl oz. It is important to remember that the Australian tablespoon differs from both the British and American tablespoons; the table below gives a comparison. The British standard tablespoon, which has been used throughout this book, holds 17·7 ml, the American 14·2 ml, and the Australian 20 ml. A teaspoon holds approximately 5 ml in all three countries.

| British | American | Australian |
|---|---|---|
| 1 teaspoon | 1 teaspoon | 1 teaspoon |
| 1 tablespoon | 1 tablespoon | 1 tablespoon |
| 2 tablespoons | 3 tablespoons | 2 tablespoons |
| $3\frac{1}{2}$ tablespoons | 4 tablespoons | 3 tablespoons |
| 4 tablespoons | 5 tablespoons | $3\frac{1}{2}$ tablespoons |

# An Imperial-American guide to solid and liquid measures

## Solid measures

| IMPERIAL | AMERICAN |
|---|---|
| 1 lb butter or margarine | 2 cups |
| 1 lb flour | 4 cups |
| 1 lb granulated or castor sugar | 2 cups |
| 1 lb icing sugar | 3 cups |
| 8 oz rice | 1 cup |

## Liquid measures

| IMPERIAL | AMERICAN |
|---|---|
| $\frac{1}{4}$ pint liquid | $\frac{2}{3}$ cup liquid |
| $\frac{1}{2}$ pint | $1\frac{1}{4}$ cups |
| $\frac{3}{4}$ pint | 2 cups |
| 1 pint | $2\frac{1}{2}$ cups |
| $1\frac{1}{2}$ pints | $3\frac{3}{4}$ cups |
| 2 pints | 5 cups ($2\frac{1}{2}$ pints) |

## Note:
When making any of the recipes in this book, only follow one set of measures as they are not interchangeable.

# Simple rules for freezing cooked food

The most important factor is that once food has been cooked it should be reduced in temperature as quickly as possible before wrapping or sealing down and stowing away in the freezer.

Do not place a pack in the freezer while it is still warm because this will cause the temperature to rise even if only very slightly and may have the effect of thawing out packages close to the new addition. Cooked food which is left exposed to the air for longer than is absolutely necessary might be contaminated or deteriorate very slightly when harmful bacteria have time to multiply.

If you take these few precautions the only expertise you need to acquire is in choosing the right container or wrapping for the kind of food to be frozen.

Most cooks feel reluctant to pack away their precious casseroles, pudding basins, flan tins and so on for an indefinite stay in the freezer as these are frequently in use. Therefore foil containers, pudding basins and flan cases bought especially for your freezer are recommended throughout the book. The method of lining the cooking utensil with foil and partially freezing the contents so that it makes a shaped pack is often simple and successful but it does not always work, takes time both at the freezing and defrosting stages, and my own preferred method is to use foil containers.

Re-usable rigid-based polythene containers with airtight seals provide very good protections but are a major investment if bought in quantity. Build up a collection of shapes and sizes you personally find useful, store carefully when not in use and they will last for many years. Of course you cannot reheat food in these containers except in some cases in a microwave oven, but many cooked foods are intended to be served cold or can easily be turned into a saucepan for reheating. Another point in favour of these containers is that they stack neatly and make the most of your precious freezer space.

Sheet foil can be used to make parcels, but the foil itself is not often in a good enough condition afterwards to be used again for a freezer pack. Double-thickness plastic cling film, recommended for use in the freezer is disposable and although it does not make quite such a firm and rigid pack as foil it still gives good protection. For short storage periods ordinary kitchen cling film can be used.

Polythene bags used with twist ties are extremely efficient and can easily be shaped by placing in preformers if the food to be frozen requires keeping in a certain shape. Even more useful are boiling and roasting bags because only one process is necessary. The prepared food is placed in the boiling bag for freezing and the bag transferred from the freezer to a saucepan of boiling water for the contents to defrost, perhaps even partially cook, and reheat. Roasting bags can be placed in dry heat in the oven.

It is important with all freezer packs to eliminate unnecessary air pockets but to leave a headspace for foods with a high water content to expand.

Defrosting is often recommended to be done in the refrigerator where the food will benefit from thawing slowly and remaining cold, or at room temperature where the only object is to thaw the food as quickly as possible.

# Home-baked breads and scones

Many housewives who have never experimented with making their own bread before become experts once they have acquired a freezer. Home-baking is not difficult and produces a considerable yield for the effort involved. Many variations are possible from a basic batch of dough. Try any of these recipes and see how much more you can produce than a simple loaf.

## Basic bread rules
The first recipe is for a simple basic white bread dough, but since so many people today prefer brown bread for health reasons, the same recipe works just as well with equal proportions of strong white flour and wholemeal flour. Quantities of risen dough required to produce stated amounts of bread are given in this recipe, as are first and second rising times. Use these instructions as a guide for all yeast recipes.

## Dried or fresh yeast
Dried yeast is freely available and has been used for these recipes. If you prefer to use fresh yeast, 25 g/1 oz fresh yeast = 15 g/½ oz dried yeast. It is possible to prepare bread dough and freeze it raw to be baked later, but this book recommends the easy straight-forward method of making and baking at the same time.

A large loaf can be defrosted, still wrapped, at room temperature in 2–4 hours, according to the warmth of the atmosphere. Smaller loaves and rolls defrost in 1–2 hours. To make a loaf crisp, unwrap and place the defrosted loaf in a moderately hot oven (200°C, 400°F, Gas Mark 6) for 5–10 minutes, according to size. If you need the bread quickly, wrap the frozen loaf in foil and bake for a further few minutes. To defrost and crisp frozen rolls, spread them out on a baking sheet and place in a moderately hot oven as above for 10 minutes. If you are watchful and remember to turn them frequently, you can also defrost rolls under the grill.

## Variety breads
Bread mixes are very easy to make up and are an encouragement to try out something a little more complicated than the basic loaf. However, the same rules apply for defrosting. Take care if you make rye bread not to harden it by oven defrosting and crisping as the texture is already very dry and firm. Enriched bread doughs produce all sorts of sweet treats and may save you money on cakes as well as at the baker's shop. They are frequently deliciously sticky, so take extra trouble to pack them for freezing in layers with dividers. Unpack while still frozen and arrange on a plate to defrost so that they look their best.

## Teabreads and scones
Breads and scones without yeast are ideal for quick preparation because there is no pause for rising. The result can be sweet or savoury and nothing is nicer than a plain teabread or scone to be spread with butter and topped with some sort of preserve. Teabreads should remain moist and are best defrosted in the sealed packs without trying to hasten matters by putting them in the oven. Unless special instructions are given, a good general rule is to serve scones slightly warm as if freshly baked, so it is always wise slightly to underbake them before freezing to avoid any danger of the tops becoming overbrown at serving time.

# Basic breads

## Basic white bread dough

### Makes approximately 2·5 kg/5½ lb dough

METRIC/IMPERIAL

| | |
|---|---|
| 1 teaspoon sugar | 1·5 kg/3 lb strong white |
| 900 ml/1½ pints warm | flour |
|   water | 4 teaspoons salt |
| 1 tablespoon dried yeast | 75 g/3 oz butter |

1 Dissolve the sugar in the warm water and sprinkle on the dried yeast. Leave for about 10 minutes until frothy.
2 Meanwhile, sift the flour and salt into a mixing bowl and rub in the butter. Add the yeast liquid and mix with the hand until a firm dough is obtained which leaves the sides of the bowl clean.
3 Turn the dough on to a floured surface and knead for about 10 minutes, until the dough is smooth and elastic.
4 Return the dough to the mixing bowl and cover with greased polythene. Allow to rise in a warm place until double in bulk.

### First rising times
1 hour in a warm place
2 hours at room temperature
12 hours in a cold room
24 hours in a refrigerator

### Hint:
Refrigerator risen dough must be returned to room temperature before shaping.

### Quantities of risen dough required for loaves and rolls
500 g/1 lb 2 oz dough for 450-g/1-lb loaf tins
1 kg/2 lb 3 oz dough for 1-kg/2-lb loaf tins
450 g/1 lb dough for a plaited loaf
50 g/2 oz dough for a medium-sized roll, any shape
350 g/12 oz dough for a crown loaf, made in a 15·5-cm/7-inch sandwich tin
100 g/4 oz dough for a 15–17·5 cm/6–7 inch pizza
225 g/8 oz dough for a 20–22·5 cm/8–9 inch pizza
450 g/1 lb dough for fruited breads made in 450-g/1-lb loaf tins

### Second rising or proving times

*Loaves in tins*
45 minutes – 1 hour in a warm place
1–1½ hours at room temperature
12 hours in a cold place
24 hours in a refrigerator

*Shaped loaves on baking sheets, or crown loaf*
45 minutes in a warm place
about 1 hour at room temperature
12 hours in a cold place
24 hours in a refrigerator

*Rolls*
30–35 minutes at room temperature

5 Turn out on a floured surface and knead again to knock out the air bubbles.

### White bread loaves
**Coburg:** Shape the dough into a ball and place on a greased baking sheet. Cut the top deeply with a sharp knife to form a cross. Brush all over with melted butter and allow to rise before baking in a hot oven (230°C, 450°F, Gas Mark 8) for about 35 minutes.

**Bloomer:** Shape the dough into a long oval shape and slash the top diagonally 4 times. Brush with beaten egg. Allow to rise before baking in a hot oven (230°C, 450°F, Gas Mark 8) for about 35 minutes.

**Tin loaf:** Shape the dough into a long oblong and roll up from the short side. Place in a greased 1-kg/2-lb loaf tin and tuck the ends underneath neatly. Score the top of the loaf along its length with a sharp knife. Allow to rise before baking in a hot oven (220°C, 425°F, Gas Mark 7) for 20 minutes. Lower heat to moderately hot (200°C, 400°F, Gas Mark 6) and bake for a further 15–20 minutes, until well browned. Rub top of loaf with butter paper and turn out of the tin to cool.

**Crisp caterpillar loaf:** Divide the dough into 5 equal pieces and shape each one into a flat round. Stack these one on top of each other and place this on its side in a greased 1-kg/2-lb loaf tin. Press down lightly to fit the tin. Brush top with water and sprinkle with cracked wheat. Allow to rise before baking in a hot oven (220°C, 425°F, Gas Mark 7) for 40–45 minutes. Turn out of tin and return to the oven for a further 5 minutes to give a crisp crust all round.

**Plaited loaf:** Divide the dough into 3 equal pieces and shape each one into a long sausage shape. Place them side by side on a greased baking sheet and plait from the centre to one end. Repeat with the other side and tuck all ends underneath neatly. Brush with salt water Allow to rise before baking in a hot oven (230°C, 450°F, Gas Mark 8) for 35–40 minutes.

**Cottage loaf:** Take off one third of the dough. Shape each piece into a round flat ball and place the larger ball on a greased baking sheet. Dampen top and place smaller piece of dough on top. Flour the handle of a wooden spoon and push down through the balls to the baking sheet. Allow to rise before baking in a hot oven (230°C, 450°F, Gas Mark 8) for 35–40 minutes.

**Crown loaf:** Divide dough into 6 pieces and shape each one into a ball. Arrange five balls to form a ring in a greased 15-cm/6-inch sandwich tin and place the sixth ball in the centre. Brush with beaten egg and sprinkle with caraway seeds. Allow to rise and bake in a hot oven (220°C, 425°F, Gas Mark 7) for 25–30 minutes.

## White bread rolls

**Catherine wheels:** Roll out 450 g/1 lb of dough thinly and cut into 8 strips about 25 cm/10 inches by 2 cm/¾ inch. Brush with melted butter and roll the strips starting at the short ends. Place cut sides up on greased baking sheets, brush with salt water and sprinkle with caraway seeds. Allow to rise before baking in a hot oven (230°C, 450°F, Gas Mark 8) for about 20 minutes.

**Twists:** Roll each piece of dough into a long sausage shape and divide in half. Twist the two pieces around each other and brush with beaten egg. Sprinkle with sesame seeds and allow to rise before baking in a hot oven (230°C, 450°F, Gas Mark 8) for about 20 minutes.

**Figure 8's:** Roll each piece of dough into a long sausage shape. Join the ends and twist into the shape of an '8'. Allow to rise then brush with melted butter and sprinkle with a little coarsely ground rock or sea salt before baking in a hot oven (230°C, 450°F, Gas Mark 8) for about 20 minutes.

**Mini plaits:** Roll each piece of dough into a long thin sausage shape and cut into 3 even pieces. Plait the pieces together. Pinch the ends together and tuck them underneath. Brush with beaten egg and allow to rise before baking in a hot oven (230°C, 450°F, Gas Mark 8) for about 20 minutes.

**Miniature cottage loaves:** Pinch off one third of each piece of dough and roll both pieces into balls. Place the larger balls on a greased baking sheet, brush tops with water and cover each one with a small ball. Flour the handle of a small wooden spoon or wooden knitting needle and push down through the dough to touch the baking sheet. Dredge very sparingly with sifted flour and allow to rise before baking in a hot oven (230°C, 450°F, Gas Mark 8) for about 20 minutes.

**Cloverleaf rolls:** Divide each piece of dough into three even portions and roll each into a ball. Place three balls together with edges touching on greased baking sheets. Brush with milk and allow to rise before baking in a hot oven (230°C, 450°F, Gas Mark 8) for 15–20 minutes.

**Finger rolls:** Shape each piece of dough into a wide sausage shape, about 10 cm/4 inches long. Allow to rise before baking in a hot oven (230°C, 450°F, Gas Mark 8) for 15–20 minutes. Brush with milk and cover with a cloth for 10 minutes to give a softer crust.

**Coburgs:** Shape each piece of dough into a ball and place on greased baking sheets. Cut the top of the ball twice with a sharp knife to make a cross. Brush with beaten egg and allow to rise before baking in a hot oven (230°C, 450°F, Gas Mark 8) for 15–20 minutes.

**Bread sticks:** Shape each piece of dough into a long thin sausage shape and place carefully on greased baking sheets. Brush with oil and allow to rise before baking in a hot oven (220°C, 425°F, Gas Mark 7) for 10 minutes. Brush with beaten egg white and sprinkle with sesame seeds and return to the oven for a further 10 minutes, until golden brown.

**Flower rolls:** Shape each piece of dough into a ball and place in a greased bun tin. Snip across the top of the balls with kitchen scissors 4 times. Brush with melted butter and allow to rise before baking in a moderately hot oven (200°C, 400°F, Gas Mark 6) for about 20 minutes.

**Fan tails:** Cut the dough into 3·75-cm/1½-inch wide strips and stack 5 strips on top of each other. Cut into 3·75 cm/1½ inch wide pieces and place cut side up in greased deep bun tins. Allow to rise before baking in a hot oven (230°C, 450°F, Gas Mark 8) for about 20 minutes.

**Crescents:** Roll 450 g/1 lb of dough into a 20-cm/8-inch circle, brush with melted butter and divide into 8 wedges. Roll each piece from the wide end to the point and twist into a crescent shape. Place on greased baking sheet, brush with melted butter and allow to rise before baking in a hot oven (220°C, 425°F, Gas Mark 7) for about 20 minutes.

**Knots:** Roll each piece of dough into a long sausage shape and tie in a single knot. Place slightly apart on a greased baking sheet, all pointing in the same direction. Brush with salt water and sprinkle with poppy seeds. Allow to rise before baking in a hot oven (230°C, 450°F, Gas Mark 8) for about 20 minutes.

**Concertinas:** Roll 450 g/1 lb of dough into a large rectangle and brush with melted butter. Fold concertina fashion along the long edge and press lightly. Cut into 8 even pieces and place in greased deep bun tins with the folds uppermost. Brush lightly with melted butter. Allow to rise before baking in a hot oven (230°C, 450°F, Gas Mark 8) for about 20 minutes.

**Parker house:** Roll out dough to 1 cm/½ inch thick and cut into 6-cm/2½-inch circles with a plain biscuit cutter. Mark in half with the blunt side of a knife not quite in the centre and fold the larger side over the smaller side until the edges are even. Brush with melted butter and sprinkle sparingly with ground nutmeg. Allow to rise before baking in a hot oven (220°C, 425°F, Gas Mark 7) for about 20 minutes.

**Mini cobs:** Shape each piece of dough into a ball. Place the balls on an unfloured surface and sprinkle a little flour in the palms of the hand. Press down hard on the rolls then ease up. Place on greased baking sheets and allow to rise before baking in a hot oven (220°C, 425°F, Gas Mark 7) for about 20 minutes.

**Wheatsheaf rolls:** Divide each piece of dough into 4 even pieces and roll each piece into a 10-cm/4-inch sausage. Place 3 strands together on a greased baking sheet and wrap the remaining strand around the middle, tucking the ends underneath. Sprinkle each roll with 1 teaspoon finely grated cheese and allow to rise before baking in a hot oven (230°C, 450°F, Gas Mark 8) for about 20 minutes.

### Hint:
If a shiny golden finish is preferred, any of these loaves or rolls can be brushed with beaten egg before baking.

## Sweet fruited bread

### Makes I small loaf

METRIC/IMPERIAL

| | |
|---|---|
| 450 g/1 lb risen white bread dough | 25 g/1 oz mixed chopped peel |
| 40 g/1½ oz seedless raisins | 2 tablespoons clear honey |
| 40 g/1½ oz sultanas | clear honey to glaze |

1 Place the dough in a bowl and gradually work in the fruit, peel and honey.
2 Turn out on a floured surface and shape to fit a greased 450-g/1-lb loaf tin.
3 Allow to rise until loaf reaches the top of tin and bake in a moderately hot oven (200°C, 400°F, Gas Mark 6) for about 30 minutes.
4 Brush top with warm clear honey to glaze.

# Bread mixes
## White bread mix loaves

### Makes 3 small loaves

METRIC/IMPERIAL

| | |
|---|---|
| scant 1 kg/1 lb 14 oz packet white bread mix | 625 ml/21 fl oz hand hot water |
| | 1 egg, beaten |

1 Place the bread mix in a mixing bowl and add the water. Work together with a wooden spoon or by hand until a soft dough is formed which leaves the sides of the bowl clean.
2 Turn out on a floured surface and knead for 5 minutes.
3 Divide the dough into three equal portions and shape each into a round bun shape. Place in greased 20-cm/8-inch sandwich tins or cake tins.
4 Cover with greased polythene and allow to rise in a warm place until double in bulk.
5 Brush with beaten egg and bake in a hot oven (230°C, 450°F, Gas Mark 8) for about 25 minutes, until the loaves are golden brown and sound hollow when tapped.

## Brown bread mix loaves

### Makes 3 small loaves

METRIC/IMPERIAL

| | |
|---|---|
| scant 1 kg/1 lb 14 oz packet brown bread mix | 25 g/1 oz butter, melted |
| 625 ml/21 fl oz hand hot water | 1 tablespoon poppy seeds |

1 Place the bread mix in a mixing bowl and add the water. Work together with a wooden spoon or by hand until a soft dough is formed which leaves the sides of the bowl clean.
2 Turn out on a floured surface and knead for 6 minutes.
3 Divide the dough into three equal portions and shape each into a long sausage shape. Curl each one into a greased 20-cm/8-inch sandwich tin or cake tin, starting at the outside edge.
4 Cover with greased polythene and allow to rise in a warm place until double in bulk.
5 Brush with melted butter and sprinkle with poppy seeds before baking in a hot oven (230°C, 450°F, Gas Mark 8) for about 25 minutes, until the loaves are brown and hollow when tapped.

### Variation:
**Quick brown nut bread:** Stir 1 teaspoon ground mixed spice into the dry bread mix before adding the water. Sprinkle 100 g/4 oz finely chopped walnuts on the floured surface and gradually work into the dough while kneading. Divide into three equal portions and shape each to fit a greased 450-g/1-lb loaf tin. Cover and allow to rise. Sprinkle with more nuts before baking in a hot oven (230°C, 450°F, Gas Mark 8) for about 25 minutes.

# Unusual breads

## Milk bread

METRIC/IMPERIAL

| | |
|---|---|
| 4 teaspoons castor sugar | 1·5 kg/3 lb strong white |
| about 600 ml/1 pint warm | flour |
| milk or milk and water | 4 teaspoons salt |
| 2 tablespoons dried yeast | 100 g/4 oz butter |
| | 2 large eggs |

1 Dissolve the sugar in the milk and sprinkle on the yeast. Allow to stand for about 10 minutes, until frothy.
2 Sift the flour and salt into a mixing bowl and rub in the butter. Add the yeast liquid and the eggs and mix to a soft dough.
3 Turn out on a floured surface and knead for about 10 minutes, until smooth and elastic.
4 Return the dough to the mixing bowl and cover with greased polythene. Allow to rise until double in bulk.
5 Turn out on a floured surface and knead again to knock out the air bubbles.
6 Shape the dough into a round flat shape and place in a greased 20-cm/8-inch cake tin. Brush the top with milk and allow to rise before baking in a moderately hot oven (200°C, 400°F, Gas Mark 6) for 40–45 minutes. After baking, cover the loaves or rolls with a cloth for 10 minutes to keep the crust soft.

**Variations:**

**Herbed milk loaf:** Work 1 tablespoon chopped fresh parsley or marjoram into the bread dough with 1 teaspoon dried mixed herbs and ¼ teaspoon garlic salt. Shape into an oblong and place in a greased 450-g/1-lb loaf tin. Brush top with salt water and sprinkle with more dried herbs. Bake in a moderately hot oven (200°C, 400°F, Gas Mark 6) for 40–45 minutes.

**Cheesed milk loaf:** Gradually work 75 g/3 oz grated strong Cheddar cheese and ¼ teaspoon celery salt into the bread dough. Shape into a round, place in a greased 20-cm/8-inch sandwich tin and slash the top three times. Brush with melted butter and bake in a moderately hot oven (200°C, 400°F, Gas Mark 6) for 35–40 minutes.

**Onion milk loaf:** Grate 1 small onion and place in a strainer to drain. Mix this into the bread dough and add ¼ teaspoon black pepper. Shape into an oblong, place on a greased baking sheet. Cut two thirds of the way through with a knife in six places along the length and fold the pieces over each other in one direction. Brush with melted butter and sprinkle top with poppy seeds. Allow to rise before baking in a moderately hot oven (200°C, 400°F, Gas Mark 6) for 35–40 minutes.

**Savoury milk bread:** Roll the dough to a large rectangle 40 cm/16 inches by 20 cm/8 inches. Cream together 1 teaspoon yeast extract spread and 25 g/1 oz butter. Spread this mixture over the dough to within 1 cm/½ inch of the edges and roll up from the short end. Place in a greased 1-kg/2-lb loaf tin and press lightly to flatten. Slash top along length and brush top with milk. Bake in a moderately hot oven (200°C, 400°F, Gas Mark 6) for 40–45 minutes.

**Milk rolls:** Shape the dough into balls and keep them as perfectly round as possible. Place well apart on a greased baking sheet and brush with milk. Bake in a hot oven (220°C, 425°F, Gas Mark 7) for 15–20 minutes, until pale golden brown.

**Creamy cheese rolls:** Roll 450 g/1 lb dough into a 25-cm/10-inch circle and divide into 8 even wedges. Roll each piece of dough slightly thinner. Mix together 75 g/3 oz cream cheese and 1 teaspoon sweet paprika pepper. Spread this mixture in the centres of the pieces of dough and roll them up from the long edge towards the point. Shape into crescents and arrange on a greased baking sheet with the points underneath. Dust tops with a little more paprika if liked and allow to rise before baking in a hot oven (220°C, 425°F, Gas Mark 7) for 15–20 minutes.

**Savoury nut rolls:** Shape 8 pieces of dough into balls then roll each out to make a 12·5-cm/5-inch circle. Mix together 50 g/2 oz finely chopped or ground salted peanuts and 50 g/2 oz finely grated Cheddar cheese. Divide this mixture between the dough circles then gather up the dough and reform into balls, completely enclosing the filling. Place with the seals downwards in greased bun tins. Brush tops with milk and sprinkle with a little more grated cheese. Allow to rise before baking in a hot oven (220°C, 425°F, Gas Mark 7) for 15–20 minutes.

## Potato bread

Makes 1 loaf

METRIC/IMPERIAL

| | |
|---|---|
| 125 ml/4 fl oz milk | 176 g/6 oz mashed |
| 1 teaspoon sugar | potato, sieved |
| 4 teaspoons dried yeast | 75 g/3 oz butter, melted |
| 350 g/12 oz plain flour | 2 eggs |
| 1 teaspoon salt | |

1 Scald the milk and allow to cool until warm. Dissolve the sugar in the milk and sprinkle on the yeast. Allow to stand for about 10 minutes, until frothy.
2 Sift the flour and salt. Combine the potato, melted butter and eggs in a large mixing bowl and gradually work in the yeast liquid and dry ingredients.
3 Turn out on a floured surface and knead for about 8 minutes, until smooth and elastic.
4 Return to the mixing bowl, cover with greased polythene and allow to rise until double in bulk.
5 Turn out on a floured surface and knead again for 2 minutes.
6 Shape the mixture into a long sausage shape and place in a greased 22·5-cm/9-inch ring cake tin. Seal the ends together and press down lightly. Allow to rise before baking in a moderately hot oven (190°C, 375°F, Gas Mark 5) for about 30 minutes.

**Variations:**

**Caraway potato loaf:** Work 1 teaspoon caraway seeds into the potato bread dough and shape the loaf into a long oblong. Roll up and place in a greased 1-kg/2-lb loaf tin. Sprinkle with more caraway seeds and allow to rise before baking in a moderately hot oven (190°C, 375°F, Gas Mark 5) for 30–35 minutes.

**Potato bread dinner rolls:** Divide the potato bread dough into 12 equal pieces and roll each into a ball. Place the balls in rows in a greased square 22·5-cm/9-inch cake tin. Brush the tops with melted butter and slash the tops of each ball once keeping the cuts running in the same direction. Brush with melted butter and allow to rise before baking in a moderately hot oven (200°C, 400°F, Gas Mark 6) for about 35 minutes. Pull apart to eat.

**Cheesed potato bread rolls:** Work 50 g/2 oz finely grated strong Cheddar cheese and 1 teaspoon dry mustard into the potato bread dough. Divide the mixture into 50-g/2-oz pieces and shape into ovals. Place well apart on the greased baking sheet, brush with egg wash. Allow to rise before baking in a moderately hot oven (200°C, 400°F, Gas Mark 6) for about 30 minutes.

# Speckled bran bread

**Makes 2 large loaves**

METRIC/IMPERIAL

| | |
|---|---|
| 2 teaspoons sugar | 2 teaspoons salt |
| 900 ml/1½ pints warm water | 225 g/8 oz unprocessed natural bran |
| 4 teaspoons dried yeast | 25 g/1 oz lard |
| 1·25 kg/2½ lb strong white flour | little cracked wheat |

1 Dissolve the sugar in the warm water and sprinkle on the yeast. Allow to stand in a warm place for about 10 minutes, until frothy.
2 Sift the white flour and salt into a mixing bowl and stir in the bran. Rub in the lard.
3 Pour the yeast liquid into the dry ingredients and mix to a soft dough. Turn out on a floured surface and knead for 10 minutes, until the dough is firm and elastic.
4 Return to the mixing bowl and cover with greased polythene. Allow to rise until double in bulk. Turn out on a floured surface and knead again for 2 minutes.
5 Divide the dough in half and shape each portion into an oblong the same width as a 1-kg/2-lb loaf tin. Fold in three and place in the greased tin. Brush the tops with salt water and sprinkle with cracked wheat.
6 Bake in a hot oven (230°C, 450°F, Gas Mark 8) for about 35 minutes.

**Variation:**

**Bran rolls:** Divide the dough into 50-g/2-oz pieces and shape each into a round ball. Roll slightly to flatten then snip round the edge six times with kitchen scissors. Place on greased baking sheets, brush with beaten egg and bake in a hot oven (230°C, 450°F, Gas Mark 8) for about 20 minutes.

# Cheese and tomato bread

**Makes 2 loaves**

METRIC/IMPERIAL

| | |
|---|---|
| about 550 g/1¼ lb strong white flour | 200 ml/6 fl oz water |
| 2 tablespoons sugar | 225 g/8 oz Cheddar cheese, grated |
| 2 teaspoons salt | 2 tablespoons tomato purée |
| 6 teaspoons dried yeast | |
| 250 ml/8 fl oz milk | |

1 Place 175 g/6 oz of the flour, the sugar, salt and yeast in a large mixing bowl.
2 Mix together the milk, water, cheese and tomato purée in a saucepan and heat gently until very warm. It is not necessary for the cheese to melt.
3 Pour cheese mixture into the dry ingredients and beat very thoroughly with a wooden spoon until mixture forms a thick batter. Gradually stir in sufficient flour to make a soft dough.
4 Turn out on a floured surface and knead for about 10 minutes, until smooth and elastic.
5 Return the dough to the mixing bowl, cover with greased polythene and allow to rise until double in bulk.
6 Turn out on a floured surface and knead again for 2 minutes.
7 Return once more to the bowl, cover and allow to stand to 15 minutes.
8 Divide the dough in half and shape each piece to fit a greased 1-kg/2-lb loaf tin.
9 Allow to rise before baking in a moderately hot oven (190°C, 375°F, Gas Mark 5) for 40–45 minutes.

# Rye bread

**Makes 2 loaves**

METRIC/IMPERIAL

| | |
|---|---|
| 2 tablespoons black treacle | 450 g/1 lb rye flour |
| 900 ml/1½ pints tepid water | 1 tablespoon salt |
| 25 g/1 oz dried yeast | 25 g/1 oz butter |
| 1 kg/2 lb wholewheat flour | 1 egg, beaten |

1 Dissolve 1 tablespoon of the treacle in 300 ml/½ pint tepid water. Sprinkle on the yeast and allow to stand for about 10 minutes until frothy.
2 Place the flours and salt in a mixing bowl and rub in the butter. Pour in the yeast liquid and the remaining water and treacle and mix to a soft dough.

3 Turn out on a floured surface and knead for 5 minutes.
4 Return the dough to the mixing bowl, cover with greased polythene and allow to rise until double in bulk.
5 Turn out on a floured surface and knead again for 2 minutes.
6 Divide into 2 portions, shape each into a long sausage shape and place on greased baking sheets. Slash the top of each loaf diagonally several times and brush all over with beaten egg.
7 Bake in a hot oven (230°C, 450°F, Gas Mark 8) for 20 minutes, reduce heat to moderately hot (200°C, 400°F, Gas Mark 6) and bake for a further 20 minutes.

3 Pour liquid into the flour mixture and beat very thoroughly with a wooden spoon until the mixture forms a thick batter. Gradually stir in sufficient flour to form a soft dough.
4 Turn out on a floured board and knead for about 10 minutes, until firm and elastic.
5 Return to the mixing bowl, cover with greased polythene and allow to rise until double in bulk.
6 Turn out on a floured surface and knead again for 2 minutes.
7 Return once more to the bowl, cover and allow to stand for 15 minutes.
8 Divide the dough in half and shape each piece into a large oblong. Roll up from the short ends and place each roll in a greased 1-kg/2-lb loaf tin. Brush with salt water and sprinkle with more oats.
9 Allow to rise before baking in a moderate oven (180°C, 350°F, Gas Mark 4) for about 50 minutes.

## Easy black bread

**Makes I loaf**

METRIC/IMPERIAL

| | |
|---|---|
| 275 g/10 oz white bread mix | 3 tablespoons gravy browning |
| 150 ml/5 fl oz boiling water | I tablespoon black treacle little melted butter |

1 Place the bread mix in a mixing bowl.
2 Mix together the water, gravy browning and black treacle and allow to cool until just bearable to the hand.
3 Pour liquid into the dry ingredients and mix well until a smooth dough is formed.
4 Turn out on a floured surface and knead for 5 minutes.
5 Form the dough into a round bun shape and place on a greased baking sheet. Cover with a bowl and allow to rise for 2–3 hours, until double in size. Slash across the top deeply several times and brush all over with melted butter.
6 Bake in a hot oven (230°C, 450°F, Gas Mark 8) for 30–40 minutes.

## Oaty bread

**Makes 2 loaves**

METRIC/IMPERIAL

| | |
|---|---|
| about 0·5 kg/1¼ lb strong white flour | 475 ml/16 fl oz water |
| 2 tablespoons salt | 25 g/1 oz butter |
| 4 teaspoons dried yeast | 100 g/4 oz golden syrup |
| | 100 g/4 oz rolled oats |

1 Mix together 225 g/8 oz of the flour, the salt and dried yeast.
2 Combine the water, butter, syrup and oats in a saucepan and heat gently until very warm. It is not necessary for the fat to melt.

## No-knead Granary loaf

**Makes 4 loaves**

METRIC/IMPERIAL

| | |
|---|---|
| 1·5 kg/3½ lb coarse whole wheat flour | 25 g/1 oz dark brown sugar or 2 tablespoons black treacle |
| 2 teaspoons salt | |
| 25 g/1 oz fresh yeast | 1·25 litres/scant 2¼ pints tepid water |

To make this bread successfully it is necessary to warm the mixing bowl with the flour and salt in it, and 2 × 1-kg/2-lb and 2 × 450-g/1-lb greased loaf tins.
2 Cream the yeast in a small basin, sprinkle on the sugar and add 150 ml/¼ pint of the water. Allow to stand for about 10 minutes, until frothy. Stir well.
3 Pour the yeast liquid into the flour mixture with the remaining water. Mix well with a wooden spoon to make a wet dough.
4 Spoon into the prepared loaf tins and cover with cloths. The loaves must stand in a warm place for about 20 minutes – until risen by about one third. To do this either put them in an electric oven while it is heating up, or in the top of a cool gas oven. After this time, remove the cloths.
5 Bake in a moderately hot oven (190°C, 375°F, Gas Mark 5) for 35–40 minutes for the smaller loaves and 45–50 minutes for the larger loaves.

**Hint:**
It is better to use fresh yeast if possible for **Granary** bread. If unobtainable substitute 1 tablespoon dried yeast and sprinkle over the liquid with the sugar in it.

# Enriched breads

## Enriched bread dough

(no dissolve method)

METRIC/IMPERIAL

| | |
|---|---|
| about 1 kg/2 lb plain flour | 350 ml/12 fl oz milk |
| 225 g/8 oz sugar | 125 ml/4 fl oz water |
| 1 teaspoon salt | 225 g/8 oz butter, diced |
| 4 teaspoons dried yeast | 2 eggs |
| 1 tablespoon finely grated lemon rind | |

1 Mix together 225 g/8 oz of the flour with the sugar, salt, yeast and lemon rind.
2 Combine the milk, water and butter until very warm. It is not necessary for the butter to melt. Pour this into the dry ingredients with the eggs and beat very thoroughly with a wooden spoon until the mixture forms a thick batter. Gradually stir in sufficient flour to make a soft dough.
3 Turn out on a floured surface and knead for about 10 minutes, until smooth and elastic.
4 Return to the mixing bowl, cover with greased polythene and allow to rise until double in bulk.
5 Turn out and knead again for about 2 minutes. Return to the bowl, cover and allow to stand for a further 15 minutes.
6 This dough can be used to make any of the following variations.

### Variations:

**Sugar whirls:** Roll out one third quantity of enriched bread dough into a large oblong. Brush surface with melted butter. Roll up from the long side like a Swiss roll. Cut 2-cm/¾-inch slices from the roll and arrange on greased baking sheets, cut side up. Allow to rise before baking in a moderate oven (180°C, 350°F, Gas Mark 4) for about 20 minutes, until golden brown. Sprinkle with crushed lump sugar while still hot.

**Cranberry date pinwheels:** Roll out one third quantity of enriched bread dough into an oblong 40 cm/16 inches by 30 cm/12 inches. Spread with 175 g/6 oz cranberry sauce and sprinkle with 100 g/4 oz chopped stoned dates. Roll up from the long edge to make a roll and seal the edge. Cut into 12 slices and arrange these, cut side up, in a greased 20-cm/8-inch square cake tin. Cover and allow to rise until double in size before baking in a moderate oven (180°C, 350°F, Gas Mark 4) for about 25 minutes, until golden brown on top. Pull apart to eat.

**Raspberry jam rosebuds:** Roll out one third quantity of enriched bread dough into an oblong 40 cm/16 inches by 30 cm/12 inches. Spread with 225 g/8 oz raspberry jam. Roll up from the long edge to make a roll and seal the edge. Cut into 12 slices and arrange these, cut side up, in greased deep bun tins. Cut across the tops twice with kitchen scissors to give a rosebud effect. Cover and allow to rise until double in size before baking in a moderately hot oven (190°C, 375°F, Gas Mark 5) for 15–20 minutes.

**Apricot buns:** Divide one third quantity of enriched bread dough into 12 pieces. Roll out each piece to a circle. Drain and chop 12 canned apricot halves and stir in 25 g/1 oz chopped candied peel and ½ teaspoon finely grated orange rind. Divide the filling between the dough circles and fold up the edges to enclose the filling completely. Seal the edges well together. Place the buns on a greased baking sheet, cover and allow to rise until double in size before baking in a moderately hot oven (190°C, 375°F, Gas Mark 5) for 15–20 minutes. Drizzle with glacé icing while still warm.

**Spicy fruit plait:** Take one half quantity of enriched bread dough and divide into three equal pieces. Roll out each piece to a long strip 30 cm/12 inches by 10 cm/4 inches. Mix together 50 g/2 oz chopped glacé cherries, 50 g/2 oz currants, 50 g/2 oz chopped candied peel and 2 teaspoons ground cinnamon. Spread this mixture down the centres of the dough strips. Fold over and seal the long edges together to make three rolls. Plait the rolls loosely together, tuck the ends underneath and place the plait on a greased baking sheet. Allow to rise until double in size before baking in a moderate oven (180°C, 350°F, Gas Mark 4) for about 35 minutes, until golden brown. Brush with warm clear honey while still hot.

**Iced cherry ring:** Take one third quantity of enriched bread dough and roll out to an oblong 30 cm/12 inches by 20 cm/8 inches. Mix together 25 g/1 oz butter, 50 g/2 oz castor sugar, 50 g/2 oz sultanas, a pinch of ground cloves and ½ teaspoon ground nutmeg. Spread this filling over the dough, leaving a border 2·5 cm/1 inch wide down one long side. Roll up tightly from the other long side and seal the plain edge with beaten egg. Place the roll on a greased baking sheet, twist to form a circle and seal the ends together. Cut with a pair of kitchen scissors from the outside two thirds through the ring towards the centre at 2·5-cm/1-inch intervals all round. Spread out the cut portions, cover and allow to rise until double in size before baking in a moderately hot oven (190°C, 375°F, Gas Mark 5) for about 30 minutes. While still warm, decorate the ring with glacé icing and arrange halved glacé cherries on the top.

**Almond loaf:** Roll out one third quantity of enriched bread dough into a rectangle 30 cm/12 inches by 22·5 cm/9 inches. Beat together 25 g/1 oz butter, 50 g/2 oz castor sugar, 50 g/2 oz ground almonds and ½ teaspoon almond essence. Spread this over the dough and roll up starting from one short edge. Place the roll, seal downwards, in a greased 1-kg/2-lb loaf tin. Cover and allow to rise until double in size then brush with beaten egg. Bake in a moderate oven (180°C, 350°F, Gas Mark 4) for about 35 minutes, until golden brown on top. Ice top with almond-flavoured glacé icing and sprinkle with flaked almonds.

# Simple coffeecake

### Makes I cake

METRIC/IMPERIAL

225 g/8 oz self-raising
  flour
½ teaspoon salt
100 g/4 oz castor sugar
75 g/3 oz butter
I egg, beaten

scant 150 ml/¼ pint milk
50 g/2 oz chopped mixed
  nuts
2 tablespoons brown sugar
I teaspoon ground
  cinnamon

1 Sift the flour and salt into a bowl and stir in the castor sugar. Rub in the butter and add the egg and sufficient milk to make a soft dough.
2 Turn the mixture into a well-greased 22·5-cm/9-inch cake tin and level the top. Mix together the nuts, brown sugar and cinnamon and sprinkle over the dough.
3 Bake in a moderately hot oven (200°C, 400°F, Gas Mark 6) for about 25 minutes, until well risen and firm to the touch. Cool on a wire rack.

### Variations:

**Apple and orange coffeecake:** Place half the dough in the prepared tin and cover with 1 large cooking apple, peeled, cored and sliced. Sprinkle this with 1 tablespoon grated orange rind and 2 tablespoons demerara sugar. Cover with the remaining dough and sprinkle the top with a little more sugar. Bake in a moderately hot oven, as above, for about 35 minutes.

**Sweet cherry coffeecake:** Finely chop 100 g/4 oz glacé cherries. Place half the dough in the prepared tin and cover with half the chopped cherries. Cover with the remaining dough and sprinkle the remaining chopped cherries over the top. Bake in a moderately hot oven, as above, for about 30 minutes. Drizzle top with glacé icing when cool.

# Spicy apple loaf

### Makes 3 small loaves

METRIC/IMPERIAL

450 g/I lb plain flour
2 teaspoons ground
  cinnamon
½ teaspoon ground nutmeg
½ teaspoon ground cloves
450 g/I lb smooth apple
  purée

½ teaspoon salt
2 teaspoons bicarbonate
  of soda
100 g/4 oz butter
225 g/8 oz castor sugar
2 eggs, beaten

1 Sift the flour with the spices, salt and soda.
2 Cream the butter and sugar until light and fluffy. Gradually beat in the eggs and fold in the dry ingredients, with the apple purée.
3 Turn into three well-greased 450-g/1-lb loaf tins and bake in a moderate oven (180°C, 350°F, Gas Mark 4) for about 1 hour. Cool on a wire tray.

# Nut and spice batter cake

METRIC/IMPERIAL

275 g/10 oz self-raising
  flour
I teaspoon baking powder
I teaspoon bicarbonate of
  soda
225 g/8 oz butter
350 g/12 oz sugar
3 eggs

I teaspoon vanilla essence
300 ml/½ pint soured
  cream
225 g/8 oz finely chopped
  nuts
2 teaspoon ground
  cinnamon

1 Sift the flour, baking powder and bicarbonate of soda.
2 Cream the butter with 275 g/10 oz of the sugar until light and fluffy. Gradually beat in the eggs and fold in the sifted flour mixture with the vanilla essence and soured cream.
3 Pour half this mixture into a greased 22·5-cm/9-inch loose-bottomed cake tin. Mix together the nuts, cinnamon and remaining sugar and sprinkle half over the batter mixture. Cover with the rest of the batter and sprinkle the remaining nut mixture over the top.
4 Bake in a moderate oven (180°C, 350°F, Gas Mark 4) for about 1 hour.
5 After freezing, defrost and reheat in a moderate oven as above for 20 minutes.

### Variation:

**Fruity batter cake**

Use 100 g/4 oz finely chopped glacé cherries and 100 g/4 oz sultanas instead of the nut and spice mixture.

# Danish pastry dough

### Makes about I6 pastries of any shape

METRIC/IMPERIAL

450 g/I lb plain flour
2 teaspoons salt
25 g/I oz lard
I teaspoon sugar
about 250 ml/8 fl oz
  warm water

I tablespoon dried yeast
I egg
175 g/6 oz hard margarine

1 Mix together the flour and salt. Rub in the lard.
2 Dissolve the sugar in the water and sprinkle on the yeast. Allow to stand for about 10 minutes, until frothy.
3 Add liquid to the dry ingredients with the egg.
4 Turn out on a floured board and knead for about 10 minutes, until smooth and elastic. Roll out to a strip about 50 cm/20 inches by 20 cm/8 inches and 5 mm/¼ inch thick, keeping the edges straight.
5 Divide the margarine into three equal portions and use one portion to dot over two thirds of the dough. Fold in three by bringing up the plain bottom third first, then folding the top third over. Give the dough a one quarter turn to the right, seal the open edges with a rolling pin then press the dough at intervals with the rolling pin.

6 Roll out again and repeat the dotting, folding and turning process twice.
7 Cover with greased polythene and chill in the refrigerator for 30 minutes.
8 Repeat the rolling and folding process three more times.
9 Cover again and chill for a hour before shaping. Alternatively, chill overnight for shaping the following day or freeze.

This dough can be used to make any of the following variations.

**Hint:**
To make a large batch of Danish pastries for freezing, it is much easier to make the basic quantity twice, folding and rolling the second batch while the first is chilling in the refrigerator and so on. A larger batch of dough is difficult to handle in bulk.

**Variations:**
**Gingernut stars:** Mix together 50 g/2 oz finely chopped hazelnuts, 2 tablespoons finely chopped preserved ginger and 2 teaspoons ginger syrup from the jar. Roll out one half quantity of the Danish pastry dough thinly and cut into 7·5-cm/3-inch squares. Divide the filling among the squares and make a cut in the pastry from each corner towards the centre of the square. Fold one corner of each section into the centre, press firmly and cover with a slice of preserved ginger.

**Cinnamon lemon cushions:** Beat together 50 g/2 oz butter, 50 g/2 oz castor sugar, 2 teaspoons ground cinnamon and ½ teaspoon finely ground lemon rind. Roll out one half quantity of the Danish pastry dough thinly and cut into 7·5-cm/3-inch squares. Divide the cinnamon filling among the squares and fold in two opposite corners of the pastry to meet in the centre. Press firmly.

**Almond paste combs:** Beat together 25 g/1 oz butter, 75 g/3 oz castor sugar, 75 g/3 oz ground almonds, 1 beaten egg and ½ teaspoon almond essence. Roll out one half quantity of the Danish pastry dough and cut into 10-cm/4-inch squares. Divide the almond filling between the squares and spread on one half of the pastry. Fold the plain piece over the top and seal the edges with beaten egg. Make four cuts in the folded edge of each pastry and open out the cuts slightly.
Place the shaped and filled pastries on greased baking sheets, cover with greased polythene and allow to prove until risen by half. Brush with beaten egg white and bake in a hot oven (220°C, 425°F, Gas Mark 7) for 20–30 minutes, until golden brown. Brush with thin glacé icing or warm honey while still hot and sprinkle with chopped nuts if liked.

# Non-yeasted breads

## Banana and cottage cheese teabread

**Makes I large loaf**

METRIC/IMPERIAL

| | |
|---|---|
| 225 g/8 oz self-raising flour | 3 eggs |
| I teaspoon baking powder | 50 g/2 oz sultanas |
| 225 g/8 oz cottage cheese | I large or 2 small bananas, chopped |
| 100 g/4 oz soft brown sugar | |

1 Sift the flour and baking powder together.
2 Cream the cheese and sugar and gradually beat in the eggs. Stir in the sultanas and banana then fold in the dry ingredients.
3 Turn into a greased and lined 1-kg/2-lb loaf tin and bake in a moderate oven (180°C, 350°F, Gas Mark 4) for 40–45 minutes, until golden brown and firm to the touch. Turn out after 5 minutes and cool on a wire tray.

## Apricot tea loaf

**Makes I large loaf**

METRIC/IMPERIAL

| | |
|---|---|
| 215 g/7½ oz self-raising flour | 100 g/4 oz dried apricots, chopped |
| 1½ teaspoons baking powder | 125 ml/4 fl oz corn oil |
| ¼ teaspoon salt | 2 tablespoons milk |
| 175 g/6 oz castor sugar | 3 eggs |
| 100 g/4 oz sultanas | ¼ teaspoon vanilla essence |

1 Sift the flour, baking powder and salt into a bowl. Add the sugar, sultanas and apricots.
2 Whisk together the oil, milk, eggs and vanilla essence. Add to the dry ingredients and beat until thoroughly mixed.
3 Pour into a greased 1-kg/2-lb loaf tin and bake in a moderate oven (160°C, 325°F, Gas Mark 3) for 1–1¼ hours, until well-risen and golden brown.
4 Allow to stand in the tin for 5 minutes then cool on a wire rack before freezing.
5 Defrost in the sealed pack.

## Nutty pineapple teabread

**Makes 2 small loaves**

METRIC/IMPERIAL

| | |
|---|---|
| 350 g/12 oz can pineapple cubes | 50 g/2 oz butter |
| 450 g/1 lb plain flour | 2 eggs, beaten |
| ¼ teaspoon ground nutmeg | I tablespoon finely grated orange rind |
| 3 teaspoons baking powder | 50 g/2 oz chopped almonds |
| 150 g/5 oz soft brown sugar | |

1 Drain the pineapple cubes and halve them. Make the syrup up to 250 ml/8 fl oz with water.
2 Sift the flour, nutmeg and baking powder into a bowl and stir in the sugar.
3 Melt the butter, add to the syrup with the eggs and whisk thoroughly. Pour the liquid into the dry ingredients and beat well. Add the orange rind, pineapple and nuts.
4 Turn into two well-greased 450-g/1-lb loaf tins and bake in a moderate oven (180°C, 350°F, Gas Mark 4) for about 1 hour. Turn out after 5 minutes and cool on a wire tray.

## Fruited malt teabread

### Makes 1 large loaf

METRIC/IMPERIAL

225 g/8 oz mixed dried fruit (raisins, sultanas, currants)
1 teaspoon bicarbonate of soda
300 ml/½ pint boiling milk
50 g/2 oz margarine
50 g/2 oz malted milk drink powder

100 g/4 oz castor sugar
1 egg, beaten
275 g/10 oz self-raising flour
1 teaspoon ground mixed spice
1 teaspoon baking powder

1 Place the fruit in a basin with the bicarbonate of soda and pour over the boiling milk. Stir well and allow to stand until cool.
2 Cream the margarine, malted milk drink powder and sugar until light and fluffy. Gradually beat in the egg.
3 Sift the flour, spice and baking powder together and fold into the creamed mixture with the soaked fruit and milk.
4 Turn into a greased and lined 1-kg/2-lb loaf tin and bake in a moderate oven (160°C, 325°F, Gas Mark 3) for 1½–2 hours, until firm to the touch and nicely browned. Cool on a wire tray.

## Marmite tea loaf

An easy to make loaf with the texture of a cake. Slice it thickly and serve buttered with cold meats or egg dishes and whole tomatoes.

### Makes 1 loaf

METRIC/IMPERIAL

225 g/8 oz self-raising flour
1 teaspoon dry mustard
pinch of salt
pinch of pepper
75 g/3 oz margarine

75 g/3 oz Cheddar cheese, grated
2 teaspoons yeast extract
2 tablespoons hot water
1 egg, beaten
4–5 tablespoons milk

1 Sift the flour and mustard into a bowl. Add the salt and pepper. Rub in the margarine. Stir in the cheese.
2 Dissolve the yeast extract in the water, add to the dry ingredients with the egg and sufficient milk to form a fairly soft batter.
3 Transfer to a greased and lined 450-g/1-lb loaf tin. Bake in a moderately hot oven (190°C, 375°F, Gas Mark 5) for about 50 minutes, or until a wooden cocktail stick inserted into the centre comes out clean.
4 Cool on a wire rack and pack in a polythene bag.
5 Defrost in the sealed bag before slicing.

# Scones

## Rich tea scones

**Makes about 24 scones**

METRIC/IMPERIAL
| | |
|---|---|
| 450 g/1 lb plain flour | 50 g/2 oz butter |
| 1 tablespoon baking powder | 2 eggs, beaten |
| ¼ teaspoon salt | about 300 ml/½ pint milk |

1 Sift the flour, baking powder and salt into a bowl. Rub in the butter.
2 Add most of the beaten egg to the dry ingredients with sufficient milk to make a soft dough.
3 Turn out on a floured surface and pat out to a thickness of 2 cm/¾ inch. Cut into 5-cm/2-inch rounds and arrange on floured baking sheets. Brush with the remaining beaten egg.
4 Bake in a hot oven (230°C, 450°F, Gas Mark 8) for about 10 minutes, until well risen and golden brown.

### Variations:
**Fruited tea scones:** Add 50 g/2 oz sultanas and 1 tablespoon castor sugar to the dry ingredients before mixing. Bake as above.

**Coffee walnut scones:** Add 1 tablespoon instant coffee powder, 2 tablespoons castor sugar and 50 g/2 oz chopped walnuts to the dry ingredients before mixing. Bake as above.

## Parsley scones

**Makes about 24 scones**

METRIC/IMPERIAL
| | |
|---|---|
| 225 g/8 oz plain flour | 4 tablespoons chopped fresh parsley |
| 1 teaspoon bicarbonate of soda | 1 teaspoon dried parsley |
| 2 teaspoons baking powder | 100 g/4 oz butter |
| 1 teaspoon salt | about 300 ml/½ pint natural yogurt |
| 225 g/8 oz wholewheat flour | little milk |

1 Sift the plain flour with the bicarbonate of soda, baking powder and salt into a bowl. Stir in the wholewheat flour and the fresh and dried parsley, and rub in the butter. Add sufficient yogurt to make a soft dough.
2 Turn out on a floured surface and pat out to a thickness of 2 cm/¾ inch.
3 Cut into triangles having about 5-cm/2-inch sides, arrange on greased baking sheets and brush with milk.
4 Bake in a moderately hot oven (200°C, 400°F, Gas Mark 6) for 10–15 minutes, until well risen and golden brown.
5 Arrange on a baking sheet and reheat from frozen in a hot oven (220°C, 425°F, Gas Mark 7) for 10 minutes.

### Variation:
**Herby garlic scones:** Substitute dried mixed herbs for the dried parsley, and use garlic salt. Bake as for parsley scones.

## Oaty scones

**Makes about 24 scones**

METRIC/IMPERIAL
| | |
|---|---|
| 400 g/14 oz plain flour | 100 g/4 oz butter |
| 4 teaspoons baking powder | 100 g/4 oz whipped vegetable fat |
| 50 g/2 oz rolled oats | generous 300 ml/½ pint milk |

1 Sift the plain flour and baking powder into a bowl. Stir in the oats and rub in the butter and fat.
2 Add sufficient milk to make a soft dough.
3 Turn out on a floured surface and pat out to a thickness of 1·5 cm/½ inch. Cut into rounds with a 5-cm/2-inch fluted biscuit cutter and arrange on greased baking sheets.
4 Bake in a moderately hot oven 200°C, 400°F, Gas Mark 6 for about 10 minutes, until risen and pale golden brown.
5 Arrange on baking sheets and reheat from frozen in a moderately hot oven, as above, for about 10 minutes. Serve split, with butter and marmalade.

### Variation:
**Oaty cinnamon scones:** Add 1 teaspoon ground cinnamon with the dry ingredients before mixing. Bake as above and serve with butter and honey.

## Cheesy wholewheat scones

**Makes about 24 scones**

METRIC/IMPERIAL
| | |
|---|---|
| 225 g/8 oz plain flour | 150 g/5 oz butter |
| 4 teaspoons baking powder | 100 g/4 oz Cheddar cheese, grated |
| ½ teaspoon salt | about 300 ml/½ pint milk |
| 225 g/8 oz wholewheat flour | |

1 Sift the plain flour, baking powder and salt into a bowl. Stir in the wholewheat flour and rub in the butter and grated cheese.
2 Add sufficient milk to make a soft dough and knead lightly.
3 Turn out on a floured surface and pat out to a thickness of 1·5 cm/½ inch. Cut into 5-cm/2-inch rounds, place on well-greased baking sheets and brush with milk.
4 Bake in a hot oven (220°C, 425°F, Gas Mark 7) for about 10 minutes, until well risen and golden brown.
5 Arrange on a baking sheet and reheat from frozen in a hot oven, as above, for 10 minutes.

### Variation:
**Savoury cheese scones:** Add ½ teaspoon dry mustard with the plain flour and ¼ teaspoon Worcestershire sauce with the milk for mixing. Bake as above.

# Mincemeat squares

## Makes 32 squares

METRIC/IMPERIAL

| | |
|---|---|
| 225 g/8 oz self-raising flour | about 150 ml/¼ pint water |
| ¼ teaspoon salt | 450 g/1 lb mincemeat |
| 150 g/5 oz lard | 1 egg, beaten |

1 Sift the flour and salt into a bowl. Cut in the lard with a knife but do not rub in with the fingers.
2 Add sufficient cold water to make a stiff paste.
3 Turn out on a floured surface and roll to a long narrow strip. Fold this into three, turn one of the open ends towards you and roll out again. Repeat the rolling, folding and turning process three times.
4 Roll out thinly to a square approximately 50 cm/20 inches, cut in half and place one piece on a greased baking sheet. Spread with the mincemeat, leaving a small border clear all the way round. Place the remaining piece of pastry on top, dampen the edges and seal well together. Brush with beaten egg.
5 Open freeze before packing. Bake from frozen in a hot oven (220°C, 425°F, Gas Mark 7) for about 30 minutes. Cut into 6-cm/2½-inch squares and sprinkle with castor sugar before serving.

# Honey ginger scones

## Makes 24 scones

METRIC/IMPERIAL

| | |
|---|---|
| 225 g/8 oz plain flour | 100 g/4 oz butter |
| 2 teaspoons ground ginger | 1 egg |
| 1 tablespoon baking powder | about 300 ml/½ pint milk |
| ¼ teaspoon salt | 2 tablespoons clear honey |
| 225 g/8 oz wholemeal flour | |

1 Sift the plain flour with the ginger, baking powder and salt into a bowl. Stir in the wholemeal flour. Rub in the butter.
2 Beat the egg with half the milk and stir in the honey. Add to the dry ingredients to form a soft dough, using as much of the remaining milk as necessary.
3 Turn out on a floured surface, divide the dough, and pat out to make two large circles. Transfer to greased baking sheets. Mark each circle to make 12 wedges with the back of a knife blade. Brush with milk.
4 Bake in a hot oven (230°C, 450°F, Gas Mark 6) for about 15 minutes, or until well risen and brown.
5 Wrap in foil or polythene bag for freezing.
6 Unwrap and arrange on a baking sheet. Reheat from frozen in a moderately hot oven (190°C, 375°F, Gas Mark 5) for about 10 minutes. Serve broken into wedges, split and buttered.

# Make-ahead main meals

A great proportion of cooked main dishes are casseroles and stews and there are a number of ways in which they can be frozen, defrosted and reheated. The choice is yours. Pack the food in rigid-based polythene containers, or polythene bags, in which case it must be turned out into a saucepan to be reheated on the hob, or into an ovenproof casserole to reheat in the oven. It may be necessary to dip the bag or container into hot water before you can release the block of food. If you use this method, gently break up the food with a fork and stir several times to ensure even defrosting and that it does not get burned. If using a saucepan, put 2 tablespoons of water into it before you add the food as a precaution against sticking and burning.

### Easy freezing and defrosting
If the stew can be frozen in the container used for reheating, this avoids one messy stage in preparation. As I have already suggested, shaped foil containers, boiling bags and roasting bags, make good substitutes for your precious casserole dishes which you may not want to keep freezer-bound for long. A 4-portion pack in a boiling bag should defrost and reheat in 40 minutes in a pan of gently boiling water. Some roasting bags will stand immersion in boiling water although the seal sometimes tends to give at the corners. Roasting bags are best used in dry heat in the oven. Place the bag on a baking sheet or in a roasting tin in a moderately hot oven (200°C, 400°F, Gas Mark 6) for 45 minutes–1 hour depending on the size of the bag and the density of the food. It is possible to defrost and reheat food in these bags at a lower temperature and for a longer time if you are using the oven for something else.

My preferred method is to defrost such cooked dishes before reheating as it is much easier to estimate the length of time required. Very dense large packs are inclined to leave an unexpected frozen portion in the centre even after prolonged exposure to heat.

### Common sense in cooking
Some items have to be treated with special care, as for example where you have whole fish with a sauce. Stirring, to break up the food, does obviously not apply because you want to keep the fish whole. If poultry and game are cooked in joints, you will prefer to keep the joints in good shape. Some cooked meat, especially beef, tends to shred if stirred too much. Where dishes are layered, they are much better packed for freezing in a container, especially a shaped foil container, which can go straight into the oven without disturbing the layers.

### Thick or thin
The defrosted dish may be thicker or thinner than you would like and the sauce or gravy can be adjusted to suit your taste immediately before serving. Add milk to thin cream sauces and stock to others. To thicken the sauce or gravy, add a little moistened cornflour, stir in well and keep the dish at simmering point for about 5 minutes to cook it completely.

# Fish

## Dutch fish cakes

### Makes 16 fish cakes

METRIC/IMPERIAL
0·75 kg/1½ lb white fish
450 g/1 lb hot mashed
  potato
50 g/2 oz butter
salt and black pepper
1 tablespoon lemon juice
2 tablespoons chopped
  parsley

100 g/4 oz Gouda cheese,
  grated
2 eggs, beaten
fresh breadcrumbs
*when serving:*
fat for frying

1 Place the fish in a saucepan and just cover with water. Poach gently until cooked. Drain well, remove skin and bones, and flake.
2 Beat the potato with the butter until smooth. Season well. Fold in the fish, lemon juice, parsley and cheese. Cool.
3 Divide the mixture into 16 equal portions and shape each into a round flat cake.
4 Dip in beaten egg and coat all over with bread-crumbs.
5 Freeze in layers with dividers.
6 Shallow fry from frozen in hot fat for about 8 minutes on each side, until crisp and golden brown.

### Variations:

**Herby fish cakes:** Substitute 2 tablespoons chopped fresh mixed herbs for the parsley, or use 1 teaspoon dried mixed herbs. Omit the cheese.

**Smoked fish cakes:** Substitute smoked whiting or cod fillet for the white fish and be discreet when adding salt. Omit the cheese if you wish.

**Tuna fish cakes:** Substitute 2 200-g/7-oz cans of tuna for the white fish and add 2 tablespoons salad cream instead of the lemon juice. Omit the cheese if you wish.

## Soused herrings

### Makes 8 portions

METRIC/IMPERIAL
8 large herrings, boned
1 medium onion,
  quartered
150 ml/¼ pint water
150 ml/¼ pint wine
  vinegar
3 tablespoons lemon juice

3 bay leaves
8 peppercorns
1 teaspoon salt
2 tablespoons chopped
  parsley
1 carrot, sliced

1 Trim the heads and fins from the fish. Wash carefully and dry on absorbent kitchen paper. Place a small piece of onion inside each fish and roll up from the head end towards the tail. Place the rolls close together in an ovenproof dish.
2 Place the water, vinegar, lemon juice, bay leaves and seasonings in a saucepan and bring to the boil. Remove from the heat and add the parsley, carrot and remaining onion. Pour over the fish.

3 Cover and cook in a cool oven (150°C, 300°F, Gas Mark 2) for about 1¼ hours. Keep covered until cool. Discard the bay leaves.
4 Freeze with the liquid.
5 Defrost in the refrigerator and serve cold.

### Variation:

**Soused mackerel:** Substitute small mackerel for the herrings and roll the fish without onion inside.

## Geordie fish pie

### Makes 4–5 portions

METRIC/IMPERIAL
450 g/1 lb smoked fish
  fillet
100 g/4 oz soft herring
  roes
300 ml/½ pint milk
25 g/1 oz butter

100 g/4 oz mushrooms,
  sliced
25 g/1 oz flour
salt and pepper
1 kg/2 lb creamed potato

1 Cut the fish into chunks and place in a saucepan with the roes. Pour over the milk and poach gently until cooked.
2 Meanwhile, melt the butter and use to sauté the mushrooms until golden. Stir in the flour and gradually add the strained liquid from cooking the fish. Bring to the boil, stirring constantly. Fold in the cooked fish and roe and season to taste. Place in a greased ovenproof dish or foil container.
3 Beat the potato until smooth and creamy, season to taste and either pipe or fork over the fish mixture in the dish.
4 Bake in a hot oven (220°C, 425°F, Gas Mark 7) for 25 minutes.
5 Freeze in the container.
6 Defrost before reheating in a moderate oven (180°C, 350°F, Gas Mark 4) for about 35 minutes. Brush the potato topping with a little oil if it looks too dry.

### Variation:

**Fish and scallop pie:** Substitute 4 cleaned and chopped scallops for the roes and add ½ teaspoon ground nutmeg to the butter for frying the mushrooms.

## Fruit-stuffed mackerel

### Makes 4 portions

METRIC/IMPERIAL
4 medium mackerel,
  boned
salt and pepper
2 dessert apples, peeled
1 medium onion, grated
1 teaspoon dried mixed
  herbs

1 tablespoon chopped
  parsley
1 teaspoon clear honey
75 g/3 oz fresh
  breadcrumbs
25 g/1 oz butter, melted

1 Trim the heads and fins from the mackerel, wash carefully and dry on absorbent paper. Sprinkle with salt and pepper inside and out.

2 Core and chop the apples and mix with the onion, herbs, honey and 50 g/2 oz of the breadcrumbs. Season to taste.

3 Use this mixture to stuff the fish and place them in a greased ovenproof dish or foil container. Sprinkle over the remaining breadcrumbs and drizzle with the butter.

4 Bake in a moderately hot oven (190°C, 375°F, Gas Mark 5) for about 30 minutes.

5 Cool before freezing in the baking container.

6 Defrost before reheating in a moderately hot oven as above for about 25 minutes.

### Variation:

Herrings with oat stuffing: Substitute large herrings for the mackerel and use rolled oats for half the breadcrumbs.

## Smoked fish and mushroom crumble

### Makes 4 portions

METRIC/IMPERIAL

| | |
|---|---|
| 450 g/1 lb smoked fish fillet | 100 g/4 oz mushrooms, sliced |
| 450 ml/¾ pint milk | 40 g/1½ oz flour |
| 40 g/1½ oz butter | salt and pepper |
| crumble: | |
| 75 g/3 oz butter | 175 g/6 oz plain flour |

1 Place the fish in a saucepan and pour over the milk. Poach gently until cooked. Drain, and reserve the liquid. Remove skin and bones from the fish, and flake. Make the liquid up to 450 ml/¾ pint again with water.

2 Meanwhile, melt the butter and use to sauté the mushrooms until golden.

3 Stir in the flour, and gradually add the milk liquid. Bring to the boil, stirring constantly. Cook 2 minutes. Fold in the fish and season to taste with pepper and a little salt if necessary. Place in a greased ovenproof dish or foil container. Cool.

4 To make the crumble, rub the butter into the flour and season to taste. Sprinkle over the fish mixture.

5 Bake in a moderate oven (180°C, 350°F, Gas Mark 4) for 45 minutes.

6 Cool and freeze in the baking container.

7 Reheat from frozen in a moderately hot oven (190°C, 375°F, Gas Mark 5) for about 1 hour.

### Variations

Smoked fish with cheese crumble: Add ½ teaspoon dry mustard to the flour for the crumble and stir in 75 g/3 oz grated Cheddar cheese before sprinkling over the fish mixture.

Coley and corn crumble: Substitute coley fillet for the smoked fish and stir 100 g/4 oz drained canned corn into the sauce with the fish. Season well with salt and pepper.

## Mushroom tuna bake

### Makes 4 portions

METRIC/IMPERIAL

| | |
|---|---|
| 25 g/1 oz butter | 200-g/7-oz can tuna, drained |
| 225 g/8 oz mushrooms, sliced | 100 g/4 oz frozen peas |
| 25 g/1 oz flour | 25 g/1 oz fresh breadcrumbs |
| 250 ml/8 fl oz chicken stock | 1 tablespoon oil |
| 150 ml/¼ pint single cream | 25 g/1 oz Cheddar cheese, grated |
| salt and pepper | |

1 Melt half the butter and use to sauté the mushrooms for 5 minutes.

2 Melt remaining butter and stir in the flour. Gradually add the stock and bring to the boil, stirring constantly. Cook for 2 minutes, stir in the cream and season to taste.

3 Flake the tuna and arrange in layers with the sauce, peas and mushrooms in a foil container.

4 Toss the breadcrumbs in the oil until golden, stir in the cheese and scatter over the tuna mixture.

5 Freeze in the container.

6 Uncover and reheat from frozen in a moderately hot oven (200°C, 400°F, Gas Mark 6) for about 50 minutes.

## Fisherman's parcels

### Makes 8 portions

METRIC/IMPERIAL

| | |
|---|---|
| 1 red or green pepper, deseeded | ½ teaspoon ground bay leaves |
| 1 large onion, chopped | 150 ml/¼ pint tomato ketchup |
| 50 g/2 oz butter | |
| 1 teaspoon garlic salt | 8 white fish steaks |
| | salt and pepper |

1 Chop the pepper and fry with the onion in the butter until soft. Stir in the garlic salt and ground bay leaves and fry for a further 2 minutes. Add the ketchup and mix well.

2 Place each fish steak on a square of greased foil, large enough to enclose it completely, and sprinkle with salt and pepper. Divide the sauce between the parcels, spooning it over the fish.

3 Fold up the foil and crimp the edges together to make airtight parcels.

4 Freeze before cooking.

5 Arrange frozen parcels on a baking sheet and cook in a hot oven (220°C, 425°F, Gas Mark 7) for about 35 minutes.

### Variations

Herby fish parcels: Add 2 tablespoons chopped parsley to the sauce with the ketchup and use ground mace instead of ground bay leaves.

Fish and mushroom parcels: Substitute 100 g/4 oz sliced mushrooms for the chopped pepper and use ground nutmeg instead of the ground bay leaves.

# Fish with bacon and tomato

## Makes 4 portions

METRIC/IMPERIAL

2 rashers bacon, derinded
1 medium onion, chopped
1 clove of garlic, crushed
1 tablespoon oil
1 teaspoon lemon rind, grated
1 tablespoon lemon juice
250 g/8 oz small tomatoes, peeled

4 tablespoons dry white wine
4 portions white fish, skinned
salt and pepper
25 g/1 oz Cheddar cheese, grated

1 Chop the bacon and fry with the onion and garlic in the oil in a frying pan until soft. Add the lemon rind and juice and stir well. Halve the tomatoes and add to the pan with the wine.
2 Place the fish portions in the sauce and poach gently for about 15 minutes until cooked.
3 Arrange the cooked fish in a foil container. Season the sauce and spoon over the fish.
4 Sprinkle with the cheese before freezing.
5 Uncover and reheat from frozen in a moderately hot oven (190°C, 375°F, Gas Mark 5) for about 40 minutes.

### Variation:

Fish with mushrooms and olives: Substitute 100 g/4 oz sliced mushrooms for half the tomatoes and fry with the bacon, onion and garlic. Stir 8 sliced stuffed green olives into the sauce before adding the fish. Omit the cheese.

# Smoked fish in onion sauce

## Makes 4 portions

METRIC/IMPERIAL

4 portions smoked fish fillet
1 large onion, grated
300 ml/½ pint milk
pepper to taste

40 g/1½ oz butter
1 teaspoon cornflour
1 tablespoon fresh breadcrumbs

1 Arrange the fish in a shallow pan and add water to cover. Bring to the boil and drain off the water. Scatter over the onion, pour in the milk and add pepper to taste. Dot the butter over the top, cover the pan and cook very gently for about 10 minutes, until the fish is cooked.
2 Lift the fish portions out of the liquid and arrange in a foil container. Moisten the cornflour with a little water and add to the cooking liquid. Bring to the boil, stirring constantly. Cook for 2 minutes and season to taste.
3 Pour the sauce over the fish and sprinkle with the breadcrumbs before freezing.
4 Uncover and reheat from frozen in a moderately hot oven (190°C, 375°F, Gas Mark 5) for about 30 minutes.

### Variation:

Smoked fish in parsley sauce: Use a small onion only and stir 3 tablespoons chopped parsley into the sauce with the moistened cornflour.

# Fish in pastry shells

## Makes 8 pies

METRIC/IMPERIAL

350 g/12 oz white fish fillet
175 g/6 oz smoked fish fillet
300 ml/½ pint milk and water
40 g/1½ oz butter

*when serving:*
beaten egg

100 g/4 oz mushrooms, sliced
15 g/½ oz flour
salt and pepper
450 g/1 lb shortcrust pastry (see page 67)

1 Place the white fish and smoked fish in a saucepan with milk and water. Poach gently until cooked, then drain well, reserving the liquid. Remove skin and bones and flake the fish.
2 Melt the butter and use to fry the mushrooms gently until soft. Sprinkle in the flour then gradually add the strained liquid from cooking the fish. Bring to the boil, stirring constantly. Fold in the fish and season to taste. Cool.
3 Roll out half the pastry and use to line 8 greased deep scallop shells.
4 Divide the filling between the pastry shells, roll out the remaining pastry and use to make lids. Dampen edges and seal well together.
5 Open freeze before packing.
6 Unwrap, place on a baking sheet and bake in a moderately hot oven (190°C, 375°F, Gas Mark 5) for about 30 minutes. Turn the pies out of their shells on to the baking sheet, brush with beaten egg and return to the oven for a further 10 minutes until golden brown.

# Fish 'n bean shells

## Makes 8 portions (8 shells)

METRIC/IMPERIAL

225 g/8 oz white fish fillet
300 ml/½ pint milk
25 g/1 oz butter
25 g/1 oz flour
¼ teaspoon ground nutmeg
1 teaspoon prepared mustard

salt and pepper
175 g/6 oz drained canned butterbeans
100 g/4 oz Gouda cheese, grated
0·75 kg/1½ lb creamed potato

1 Place the fish in a saucepan with the milk and poach gently until cooked. Drain, reserving the liquid. Remove skin and bones and flake the fish.
2 Melt the butter, stir in the flour and nutmeg and gradually add the strained milk from cooking the fish. Bring to the boil, stirring constantly, and cook for 2 minutes. Add the mustard and season to taste. Fold in the fish, butterbeans and half the cheese.

3 Divide the mixture between 8 greased deep scallop shells. Cool.
4 Beat the potato until smooth and pipe or fork around the fish mixture in the shells. Sprinkle with the remaining cheese.
5 Open freeze before packing.
6 Unwrap, arrange on a baking sheet and cook in a hot oven (220°C, 425°F, Gas Mark 7) for about 40 minutes, until heated through and golden brown on top.

3 Stir in the curry powder and cook for 2 minutes. Stir in the flour and gradually add the stock. Bring to the boil, stirring constantly. Chop the apple and add to the sauce with the coconut. Add salt to taste.
4 Pour the sauce over the fish, cover and cook in a moderate oven (180°C, 350°F, Gas Mark 4) for 40 minutes.
5 Freeze in the container.
6 Reheat from frozen in a moderately hot oven (190°C, 375°F, Gas Mark 5) for about 50 minutes.

### Variation
Cod in sweet curry sauce: Substitute 4 portions of cod fillet for the coley and add 2 tablespoons cranberry sauce with the apple before cooking. Omit the coconut if wished.

# Devilled coley casserole

**Makes 4 portions**

METRIC/IMPERIAL

| | |
|---|---|
| 4 portions coley | 4 tablespoons vinegar |
| 50 g/2 oz butter | 2 tablespoons brown |
| I medium onion, chopped | sugar |
| I tablespoon prepared | 300 ml/½ pint tomato |
| mustard | juice |
| I tablespoon | salt and pepper |
| Worcestershire sauce | |

1 Arrange the fish portions in a foil container.
2 Melt the butter and use to fry the onion gently until soft. Stir in the mustard, Worcestershire sauce, vinegar and sugar. Gradually add the tomato juice and season to taste with salt and pepper. Bring to the boil and pour over the fish.
3 Cover and cook in a moderate oven (180°C, 350°F, Gas Mark 4) for about 50 minutes.
4 Freeze in the container.
5 Defrost still sealed, then reheat in a moderately hot oven (190°C, 375°F, Gas Mark 5) for about 30 minutes.

# Mackerel with peanut apricot sauce

**Makes 4 portions**

METRIC/IMPERIAL

| | |
|---|---|
| 4 small mackerel, cleaned | 2 tablespoons apricot jam |
| 4 tablespoons peanut | 150 ml/¼ pint orange |
| butter | juice |
| salt and pepper | 50 g/2 oz butter |
| 2 tablespoons vinegar | |

1 Wash the fish and dry with absorbent paper. Spread 1 tablespoon peanut butter inside each one and sprinkle with salt and pepper. Place the fish in a greased ovenproof dish.
2 Gradually blend the vinegar into the jam, then add the orange juice and mix well. Heat gently, add the butter and stir until it has melted.
3 Pour the sauce over the fish and cook in a moderately hot oven (190°C, 375°F, Gas Mark 5) for 35 minutes.
4 Freeze in the dish (not in foil).
5 Defrost then reheat in a moderately hot oven, as above, for 30 minutes.

### Variations:
Mackerel with pineapple sauce: Omit the peanut butter, substitute pineapple juice for the orange juice and use 2 tablespoons crushed pineapple and 1 teaspoon clear honey instead of the apricot jam.

Herrings with plum sauce: Substitute 4 large herrings for the mackerel and use plum jam instead of the apricot jam. Omit the peanut butter if wished.

# Coley in curry sauce

**Makes 4 portions**

METRIC/IMPERIAL

| | |
|---|---|
| 4 portions coley | I large cooking apple, |
| 2 tablespoons oil | cored |
| 2 large onions, sliced | 25 g/I oz desiccated |
| I tablespoon curry | coconut |
| powder | salt |
| 25 g/I oz flour | |
| 450 ml/¾ pint chicken | |
| stock | |

1 Arrange the fish in a foil container.
2 Heat the oil and use to fry the onion gently until soft.

# Poultry and game

## Cidered chicken with peas

### Makes 6 portions

METRIC/IMPERIAL
2·25 kg/5 lb boiling fowl
1 medium onion,
 quartered
¼ teaspoon ground cloves
2 tablespoons lemon juice
few parsley stalks

1 chicken stock cube
300 ml/½ pint water
300 ml/½ pint dry cider
225 g/8 oz frozen peas
1 tablespoon cornflour
salt and pepper

1 Place the bird in a large saucepan with the onion, clove, lemon juice, parsley, stock cube, water and cider. (If necessary cut into serving pieces before doing this.) Bring to the boil, cover and simmer for 1½ hours, or until the bird is tender.
2 Drain and divide into portions. Place in an oven-proof dish or foil container.
3 Strain the stock and measure 450 ml/¾ pint into a saucepan. Add the peas, bring to the boil and simmer gently for 2 minutes.
4 Moisten the cornflour with cold water, add to the pan and bring back to the boil, stirring constantly. Simmer for 2 minutes and adjust the seasoning.
5 Pour the sauce over the chicken before freezing.
6 Defrost before reheating in a moderate oven (180°C, 350°F, Gas Mark 4) for about 35 minutes.

## Chicken with tipsy mushrooms

### Makes 4 portions

METRIC/IMPERIAL
4 chicken portions
salt and pepper
1 tablespoon sweet
 paprika pepper
3 tablespoons oil
225 g/8 oz button
 mushrooms
150 ml/¼ pint dry cider

1 teaspoon
 Worcestershire sauce
1 teaspoon cornflour
2 tablespoons evaporated
 milk
1 tablespoon chopped
 parsley

1 Rub the chicken on both sides with salt and the paprika. Fry in the oil for about 25 minutes, turning once, until golden brown and cooked through.
2 Meanwhile, trim the mushroom stalks level with the caps. Place the mushrooms in a saucepan with the cider and Worcestershire sauce and poach gently for 5 minutes.
3 Moisten the cornflour with the evaporated milk and add to the pan. Bring to the boil, stirring constantly. Simmer for 2 minutes and adjust the seasoning. Stir in the parsley.
4 Pack the chicken with the sauce in 2 boiling bags.
5 Defrost before reheating the bags in a pan of boiling water for 30 minutes.

## Californian chicken

### Makes 4 portions

METRIC/IMPERIAL
1 small green pepper,
 deseeded
100 g/4 oz mushrooms,
 sliced
50 g/2 oz butter
40 g/1½ oz flour
300 ml/½ pint chicken
 stock
150 ml/¼ pint milk

1 canned red pimento,
 chopped
450 g/1 lb cooked
 chicken, diced
1 egg yolk
150 ml/¼ pint soured
 cream
salt and pepper

1 Chop the pepper finely and fry with the mushrooms in the butter until soft.
2 Stir in the flour and gradually add the stock and milk. Bring to the boil, stirring constantly. Cook for 2 minutes and add the pimento. Fold in the chicken and cook gently for 5 minutes.
3 Beat the egg yolk with the soured cream and add to the sauce. Reheat but do not allow to boil. Season to taste.
4 Freeze in a boiling bag.
5 Reheat bag from frozen in boiling water for about 25 minutes.

## Zesty orange chicken

### Makes 4 portions

METRIC/IMPERIAL
4 chicken portions
600 ml/1 pint chicken
 stock
½ teaspoon ground mace
25 g/1 oz butter

25 g/1 oz flour
2 oranges
2 tablespoons sherry
salt and pepper

1 Place the chicken portions in a saucepan with the stock and mace. Poach gently for about 30 minutes, until tender. Drain, and reserve the stock. Arrange the chicken portions in a foil container.
2 Melt the butter and stir in the flour. Gradually add the strained cooking stock and bring to the boil, stirring constantly. Simmer for 4 minutes.
3 Finely grate the rind from the oranges and squeeze the juice. Add to the sauce with the sherry and cook for a further 5 minutes. Season to taste.
4 Pour the sauce over the chicken before freezing.
5 Defrost before reheating in a moderate oven (180°C, 350°F, Gas Mark 4) for about 35 minutes.

### Variation:

**Lemon chicken with almonds:** Substitute a lemon for one of the oranges.
Roast 25 g/1 oz flaked almonds until golden and stir into the sauce with the sherry.

# Chicken and celery pot

**Makes 4 portions**

METRIC/IMPERIAL

| | |
|---|---|
| 550 g/1¼ lb boneless chicken | 4 tablespoons corn oil |
| 5 teaspoons seasoned cornflour | 1 chicken stock cube |
| 1 medium onion | 300 ml/½ pint boiling water |
| 6 sticks celery | 1 canned red pimento |

1 Cut the chicken into large neat cubes and coat in seasoned cornflour.
2 Finely chop the onion and finely slice the celery. Heat the oil in a saucepan, add the onion and celery and fry gently until soft. Add the chicken and fry gently until firm but not coloured. Dissolve the stock cube in boiling water and add to the pan. Bring to the boil, stirring constantly. Cover and simmer for 20 minutes.
3 Cut the pimento into strips and add to the pan. Moisten the remaining cornflour with a little liquid from the can of pimento and add to the pan. Bring to the boil again, stirring all the time. Cook for 2 minutes.
4 Freeze in a boiling bag.
5 Reheat frozen bag in boiling water for about 30 minutes.

## Variation:

**Cheesy chicken with celery:** After reheating, turn the hot mixture into a serving dish, stir in 100 g/4 oz grated Cheddar cheese and serve while it is melting.

# Crispy-coated peanut chicken

**Makes 4 portions**

METRIC/IMPERIAL

| | |
|---|---|
| 4 chicken portions | 50 g/2 oz salted peanuts |
| 2 tablespoons oil | 50 g/2 oz dry breadcrumbs |
| 2 tablespoons vinegar | 2 eggs beaten |
| 2 tablespoons peanut butter | oil for frying |
| 2 tablespoons seasoned flour | |

1 Place the chicken portions in a shallow dish.
2 Whisk together the oil, vinegar and peanut butter and pour over the chicken. Allow to stand in the refrigerator for 2 hours, turning once. Pat dry with absorbent paper and coat in seasoned flour.
3 Finely chop the peanuts and mix with the breadcrumbs. Dip the chicken portions in beaten egg and coat all over with the breadcrumb mixture.
4 Shallow fry for about 25 minutes, turning once, until chicken is cooked and coating is crisp and golden brown.
5 Wrap portions individually before freezing.
6 Defrost then place portions on a greased baking sheet and reheat in a moderately hot oven (200°C, 400°F, Gas Mark 6) for about 25 minutes.

## Variation:

**Chinese nutty chicken:** Substitute 1 tablespoon soy sauce for the peanut butter and use finely chopped salted cashew nuts instead of the peanuts for the coating.

# Chicken with spiced yogurt topping

**Makes 4 portions**

METRIC/IMPERIAL

| | |
|---|---|
| 4 chicken portions | 2 teaspoons French mustard |
| 150 ml/¼ pint natural yogurt | 1 teaspoon curry powder |
| 1 tablespoon Worcestershire sauce | 2 tablespoons oil |
| 1 tablespoon tomato ketchup | |

1 Place the chicken portions in an ovenproof dish or foil container and prick all over with a large darning needle or skewer.
2 Beat together the yogurt, Worcestershire sauce, ketchup, mustard and curry powder until well blended. Spread this mixture carefully over the chicken, cover and allow to stand in the refrigerator for 1 hour.
3 Drizzle the oil over the top of the chicken and bake in a moderately hot oven (190°C, 375°F, Gas Mark 5) for about 1 hour.
4 Cover the dish or container with foil before freezing but do not allow it to actually touch the chicken portions.
5 Defrost, then uncover and reheat in a moderately hot oven (200°C, 400°F, Gas Mark 6) for 30 minutes.

# Lemon and turkey blanquette

**Makes 4 portions**

METRIC/IMPERIAL

| | |
|---|---|
| 100 g/4 oz button mushrooms, sliced | 150 ml/¼ pint chicken stock |
| 3 tablespoons water | 150 ml/¼ pint single cream |
| 1 tablespoon finely grated lemon rind | 450 g/1 lb cooked turkey, diced |
| 1 tablespoon lemon juice | salt, pepper and ground nutmeg |
| 50 g/2 oz butter | |
| 25 g/1 oz flour | |

1 Place the mushrooms in a saucepan with the water, lemon rind and juice. Cook gently for 5 minutes.
2 Meanwhile, melt the butter and stir in the flour. Gradually add the stock and cream and stir over moderate heat until the mixture thickens and is smooth.
3 Add the mushrooms and cooking liquid to the sauce and stir until well blended. Fold in the turkey and season carefully with salt, pepper and nutmeg.
4 Freeze in a boiling bag.
5 Reheat frozen bag in boiling water for about 30 minutes.

**Variation:**

**Chicken blanquette with corn:** Substitute cooked chicken for the turkey and fold 100 g/4 oz drained canned corn into the sauce with the mushrooms.

## Herbed turkey with chestnuts

### Makes 4 portions

METRIC/IMPERIAL

| | |
|---|---|
| 50 g/2 oz butter | 300 ml/½ pint milk |
| 1 large onion, chopped | 1 teaspoon dried |
| 100 g/4 oz cooked | marjoram |
| chestnuts, chopped | 350 g/12 oz frozen peas |
| 25 g/1 oz flour | 450 g/1 lb cooked turkey |
| 1 chicken stock cube | salt and pepper |
| 300 ml/½ pint water | |

1 Melt the butter and use to fry the onion and chestnut gently until the onion is soft and golden brown.
2 Sprinkle in the flour and stir well. Dissolve the stock cube in the water and milk and gradually add to the pan. Bring to the boil, stirring constantly, until slightly thickened.
3 Add the marjoram and peas and bring back to the boil and simmer for 3 minutes. Fold in the cooked turkey and season to taste.
4 Freeze in a boiling bag.
5 Reheat the frozen bag in boiling water for about 30 minutes.

## Duck with pineapple sauce

### Makes 4 portions

METRIC/IMPERIAL

| | |
|---|---|
| 1 orange | 1 teaspoon |
| 2·25 kg/5 lb duck | Worcestershire sauce |
| salt and pepper | 225-g/8-oz can pineapple |
| 150 ml/¼ pint giblet stock | pieces |
| 3 tablespoons red wine | 1 tablespoon cornflour |

1 Thinly pare the rind from the orange and cut into fine shreds. Squeeze the juice.
2 Place the duck on a trivet in a roasting tin. Sprinkle with salt and pepper and roast in a moderately hot oven (200°C, 400°F, Gas Mark 6) for 2 hours. Baste the duck occasionally with the pan juices and pour off the excess fat.
3 Remove the duck, drain well, carve into portions and arrange in foil containers.
4 Skim the pan juices again to remove surplus fat and pour into a saucepan. Add the stock, wine, orange juice and Worcestershire sauce and boil steadily for

3 minutes. Add the orange shreds and drained pineapple pieces. Moisten the cornflour with 2 tablespoons pineapple syrup, add to the sauce and bring to the boil, stirring constantly, until the sauce is thick and smooth.
5 Spoon the sauce over the duck portions before freezing.
6 Defrost, uncover and then reheat in a hot oven (220°C, 425°F, Gas Mark 7) for about 25 minutes.

**Variations:**

**Duck with cherry sauce:** Substitute a 225-g/8-oz can of pitted red cherries for the pineapple and 1 tablespoon of port and 2 tablespoons of water for the red wine. Add a pinch of ground cloves with the stock when making the sauce.

**Duck with Spanish sauce:** Omit the can of pineapple and use 16 halved stuffed green olives and 1 tablespoon of liquid from the jar blended with 1 tablespoon coarse cut marmalade. Use 2 tablespoons sweet sherry and 1 tablespoon water in place of the red wine.

## Rabbit in creamy sauce

### Makes 8 portions

METRIC/IMPERIAL

| | |
|---|---|
| 2 chicken stock cubes | few parsley stalks |
| 600 ml/1 pint boiling | 6 peppercorns |
| water | 6 cloves |
| 600 ml/1 pint milk | 8 rabbit portions (thigh |
| 225 g/8 oz bacon, | if possible) |
| derinded | 50 g/2 oz butter |
| 100 g/4 oz button | 50 g/2 oz flour |
| mushrooms, chopped | salt and pepper |

1 Dissolve the stock cubes in the water in a large saucepan and add the milk. Chop the bacon and add to the pan with the mushrooms, parsley, peppercorns and cloves. Add the rabbit portions and poach gently for 1½ hours, until tender.
2 Drain the rabbit portions and remove the flesh from the bones. Strain the cooking liquid.
3 Melt the butter and stir in the flour. Gradually add the strained liquid and bring to the boil, stirring constantly. Fold in the cooked rabbit and season to taste.
4 Freeze in 2 boiling bags.
5 Reheat each frozen bag in boiling water for about 30 minutes.

**Variation:**

**Dinner party rabbit:** Substitute 300 ml/½ pint dry white wine for part of the water and stir 150 ml/¼ pint soured cream into the sauce before freezing. Season carefully.

# Mustard rabbit casserole

## Makes 8 portions

METRIC/IMPERIAL

| | |
|---|---|
| 50 g/2 oz butter | 3 large carrots, sliced |
| 2 tablespoons oil | 900 ml/1½ pints chicken |
| 2 medium onions, | stock |
| chopped | 2 tablespoons prepared |
| 4 sticks celery, sliced | mustard |
| 8 large rabbit portions | salt and pepper |
| 50 g/2 oz seasoned flour | |

1 Heat the butter and oil and use to fry the onion and celery gently until beginning to soften.
2 Meanwhile, coat the rabbit portions in seasoned flour. Add these to the pan and brown on both sides. Place rabbit, onion and celery in an ovenproof casserole with the carrot.
3 Sprinkle any remaining seasoned flour into the juices remaining in the pan and stir well. Gradually add the stock and bring to the boil stirring constantly. Add the mustard and season to taste.
4 Pour the sauce over the rabbit mixture, cover and cook in a moderate oven (160°C, 325°F, Gas Mark 3) for about 1½ hours, until the rabbit is tender.
5 Remove rabbit flesh from the bones before freezing if preferred.


# Partridges with red cabbage

## Makes 4 portions

METRIC/IMPERIAL

| | |
|---|---|
| 2 partridges or 1 pheasant | 1 medium onion, chopped |
| 2 tablespoons seasoned | 1 medium cooking apple, |
| flour | chopped |
| 2 tablespoons oil | 2 tablespoons cider or |
| 2 rashers streaky bacon, | apple juice |
| derinded | 1 teaspoon sugar |
| 450 g/1 lb red cabbage, | salt and black pepper |
| chopped | 1 bouquet garni |

1 Cut the birds into portions and coat with seasoned flour.
2 Heat half the oil and use to fry the portions until brown on all sides. Remove and keep warm.
3 Chop the bacon, add to the pan with the remaining oil and fry for 1 minute. Add the cabbage, onion and apple and fry for 3 minutes, turning all the time. Sprinkle in the cider, sugar and seasoning to taste. Mix well.
4 Place the cabbage mixture in an ovenproof casserole, put the bird portions on top, add the bouquet garni and cover tightly.
5 Cook in a cool oven (150°C, 300°F, Gas Mark 2) for 2½ hours. Remove the bouquet garni.

### Variations:

**Partridges with sauerkraut:** Substitute sauerkraut for red cabbage. Drain well before using and be discreet when adding more seasoning. If liked, add a few juniper berries to the sauerkraut mixture.

**Partridges with white cabbage:** Substitute white cabbage for red cabbage and add ½ teaspoon caraway seeds to the cabbage mixture.


# Rich game hot pot

This is an excellent recipe for using older birds which are not sufficiently tender to roast.

## Makes 4 portions

METRIC/IMPERIAL

| | |
|---|---|
| 50 g/2 oz butter | 100 g/4 oz onion, chopped |
| 1 guinea fowl or partridge | 100 g/4 oz carrot, |
| or 2 pigeons | chopped |
| salt and pepper | 300 ml/½ pint dry red wine |
| 50 g/2 oz fat bacon, | 150 ml/¼ pint beef stock |
| derinded | ground nutmeg |
| 8 silverskin pickled onions | 1 bouquet garni |
| 1 clove garlic, crushed | 1 tablespoon cornflour |

1 Melt the butter in a large saucepan and use to brown the game all over. Season with salt and pepper, cover and cook gently for 30 minutes. Carve into serving portions.
2 Meanwhile, chop the bacon and fry gently in a saucepan with the silverskin onions, garlic and chopped vegetables until golden. Pour in the wine and beef stock and season to taste with salt, pepper and nutmeg. Add the bouquet garni, cover and simmer for 45 minutes.
3 Discard the bouquet garni. Moisten the cornflour with cold water, add to the pan and bring back to the boil, stirring vigorously. Cook for 2 minutes and add the game portions.
4 Cool and freeze in a polythene container.
5 Defrost before reheating gently in a saucepan.

# Beef

## Lemon veal casserole

**Makes 8 portions**

METRIC/IMPERIAL

50 g/2 oz butter
1·25 kg/2½ lb pie veal,
  diced
salt and pepper
1 large onion, sliced
4 large carrots, sliced

2 large leeks, sliced
generous 1 litre/2 pints
  chicken stock
1 tablespoon finely grated
  lemon rind
2 tablespoons cornflour

1 Melt the butter and use to fry the veal until sealed on all sides. Place the meat in a large ovenproof casserole and sprinkle with salt and pepper.
2 Fry the onion in the remaining butter until golden brown and add to the meat with the carrots and leeks.
3 Pour the stock and lemon rind into the pan and stir well. Moisten the cornflour with cold water and add to the pan. Bring to the boil, stirring constantly. Season to taste and pour over the meat and vegetables.
4 Cover and cook in a moderate oven (180°C, 350°F, Gas Mark 4) for about 1¾ hours, or until tender.

## Beefy pigeon stew

**Makes 8 portions**

METRIC/IMPERIAL

4 tablespoons oil
1 large onion, chopped
8 pigeon breasts
100 g/4 oz bacon,
  derinded
450 g/1 lb stewing steak,
  cubed
225 g/8 oz mushrooms,
  sliced

2 tablespoons blackcurrant
  jelly
2 tablespoons lemon juice
450 ml/¾ pint beef stock
2 tablespoons cornflour
250 ml/8 fl oz red wine
salt and pepper

1 Heat the oil and use to fry the onion until soft. Add the pigeon breasts and fry on both sides until browned. Drain and place in a large ovenproof casserole.
2 Chop the bacon and add to the pan with the steak. Cook until golden brown. Add to the casserole with the mushrooms.
3 Stir the blackcurrant jelly, lemon juice and stock into any juices remaining in the pan. Blend the cornflour with the wine, add to the pan and bring to the boil, stirring constantly until smooth. Season to taste and pour over the pigeon mixture.
4 Cover and cook in a moderate oven (160°C, 325°F, Gas Mark 3) for about 1½ hours, until the steak is tender.
5 Divide the mixture equally between 2 polythene containers.
6 Defrost then turn into a saucepan and reheat very gently to boiling point. Stir carefully to avoid breaking down the pieces of pigeon and steak.

**Variation:**
**Pigeon stew with cranberries:** Substitute 175 g/6 oz fresh or frozen cranberries for the mushrooms, omit the blackcurrant jelly and add a pinch of ground cloves to the sauce.

## Beef in brown ale

**Makes 8 portions**

METRIC/IMPERIAL

4 tablespoons oil
1·25 kg/2½ lb chuck
  steak, cubed
4 medium onions, sliced
2 cloves garlic, crushed
50 g/2 oz flour

600 ml/1 pint brown ale
600 ml/1 pint water
1 bouquet garni
2 tablespoons wine
  vinegar
salt and pepper

1 Heat the oil and use to brown the meat on all sides. Add the onion and garlic and cook gently until soft.
2 Stir in the flour, then gradually add the ale and water. Bring to the boil, stirring constantly. Add the bouquet garni, vinegar and seasoning to taste.
3 Transfer to an ovenproof casserole and cook in a moderate oven (160°C, 325°F, Gas Mark 3) for 2 hours.
4 Divide into two portions before freezing.

**Variation:**
**Crusty beef in brown ale:** Place the frozen mixture in an ovenproof casserole. Spread 2 slices of malt fruit bread thickly with mild Continental mustard and cut each into 4 triangles. Arrange on the meat mixture before reheating. Cook until the topping is crisp.

## Easy beef 'n beans

**Makes 8 portions**

METRIC/IMPERIAL

2 tablespoons oil
2 medium onions, chopped
1 teaspoon mild chilli
  powder
1·25 kg/2½ lb minced beef

3 large tomatoes, chopped
425-g/15-oz can baked
  beans in tomato sauce
salt and pepper

1 Heat the oil in a saucepan and use to fry the onion and chilli powder over gentle heat until the onion is soft.
2 Add the minced beef and cook, stirring, until the meat is well coloured.
3 Add the chopped tomato and the baked beans. Season to taste, bring to the boil and cook for 10 minutes.
4 Reheat, adjust the seasoning and serve with fluffy boiled rice.

**Variations:**
**Beef 'n butterbeans:** Substitute canned butterbeans and their liquid for the baked beans and add 2 tablespoons spicy brown table sauce at the same time.

**Mexican beef 'n beans:** Substitute canned red kidney beans and their liquid for the baked beans and add to the mixture with 1 finely chopped canned red pimento.

# Beef and pork burgers

Young children who love sausages but are not yet ready for beef hamburgers particularly like this mixture which is smoother in texture.

METRIC/IMPERIAL

| | |
|---|---|
| 2 large onions | salt and pepper |
| 0·75 kg/1½ lb minced beef | ½ teaspoon ground mace |
| 0·75 kg/1½ lb pork sausagemeat | or nutmeg |

1 Finely chop the onions and combine with the beef and sausage meat. Season to taste and add the spice.
2 With floured hands, divide the mixture into 50-g/2-oz quantities and shape into round flat cakes. Freeze in stacks with dividers.
3 Grill or fry from frozen for 5 minutes each side.

### Variations:

**Surprise croquettes:** Shape as for burgers. Put a teaspoon of sweet brown pickle in the centre of each, roll in edges to cover and form a ball. Freeze in layers with dividers. Shallow fry from frozen for 8–10 minutes, turning frequently.

**Porkieballs:** Form into even-sized balls using about a rounded tablespoon of mixture for each. Roll the balls in roughly chopped salted peanuts. Freeze in layers with dividers. Shallow fry from frozen for about 8 minutes, turning frequently.

**Firework burgers:** Sprinkle 2 teaspoons curry powder over the meat mixture and work in smoothly. Shape like chipolata sausages and coat with egg wash and toasted breadcrumbs. Shallow fry from frozen for 8–10 minutes, turning frequently.

**Bomber burgers:** Shape into 15-cm/6-inch chipolata sausage shapes. Flatten half the shapes, spread with English or Continental mustard according to taste and press the other sausage shapes on top to enclose the mustard. Coat in well-seasoned flour. Pack with concertina dividers. Fry from frozen for 8–10 minutes, turning frequently. Serve in split long soft rolls with a layer of fried onion, or in buttered soft rolls.

**Soup-size meatballs:** Add double the usual quantity of mace or nutmeg to the meat mixture. Divide into 25-g/1-oz quantities and form into balls. Coat in seasoned flour and open freeze before packing in meal-size quantities. To turn a basic fairly thin vegetable soup into a meal, heat to boiling point. Crumble the bag of frozen meatballs between your hands to separate them. Drop one at a time into the boiling soup, return to the boil and simmer for 12 minutes.

**Yorkshire roundies:** Make up or defrost 1 pint Yorkshire pudding batter. Grease a roasting tin, place 8 Porkieballs in it and cook in a moderately hot oven (200°C, 400°F, Gas Mark 6) for 10 minutes. Pour in the batter, arranging the porkieballs evenly with a fork if necessary. Return to the oven and bake for a further 25 minutes.

# Tavern crumble

## Makes 8 portions (2 crumbles)

METRIC/IMPERIAL

| | |
|---|---|
| 1 kg/2 lb chuck steak, cubed | 1 tablespoon Worcestershire sauce |
| 2 large onions, chopped | salt and pepper |
| 2 cloves garlic, crushed | 1 tablespoon cornflour |
| 4 large carrots, sliced | 100 g/4 oz butter |
| 600 ml/1 pint lemonade shandy | 225 g/8 oz plain flour |
| 300 ml/½ pint beef stock | 100 g/4 oz Cheddar cheese, grated |

1 Place the steak in an ovenproof casserole and sprinkle the onion, garlic and carrot on top. Pour over the shandy, cover and allow to stand in the refrigerator for 2 hours.
2 Mix together the stock and Worcestershire sauce and season to taste. Stir into the beef mixture in the casserole.
3 Cook in a moderate oven (160°C, 325°F, Gas Mark 3) for about 1½ hours, until the steak is almost tender. Moisten the cornflour with cold water, stir into the casserole and return to the oven for a further 30 minutes.
4 Adjust the seasoning if necessary, cool and divide the mixture between 2 ovenproof dishes or foil containers.
5 Rub the butter into the flour until crumbly, then stir in the cheese and a little seasoning. Sprinkle over the meat mixture in the containers before freezing.
6 Defrost and then reheat in a moderately hot oven (200°C, 400°F, Gas Mark 6) for about 30 minutes.

# Basic mince curry

## Makes 12 portions when extended

METRIC/IMPERIAL

| | |
|---|---|
| 1 large onion | 1 beef stock cube |
| 25 g/1 oz beef dripping or lard | 150 ml/¼ pint boiling water |
| 1 kg/2 lb minced beef | 50 g/2 oz seedless raisins |
| 1 tablespoon flour | 1 teaspoon salt |
| 1 tablespoon hot curry powder | |

1 Very finely chop the onion. Melt the dripping, add the onion and cook gently until limp. Gradually stir in the minced beef and cook over moderate heat until it is all well coloured.

2 Mix together the flour and curry powder and sprinkle over the meat mixture. Stir well and cook for 2 minutes.
3 Dissolve the stock cube in the water and add to the meat mixture together with raisins and salt. Reduce the heat and continue stirring and cooking for 5 minutes, to produce a rather dry meat mixture.
4 Remove from the heat and divide into three equal portions. Each of these portions can be served as a dry curry for four with rice and side dishes, or can be expanded to make a spicy main dish for 4.

**Variations:**

**Spicy beef:** Make up a packet of spring vegetable soup with half the water indicated. When it is boiling turn in a defrosted portion of mince curry and 100 g/4 oz frozen green peas. Gradually break up with a fork until the mixture reaches boiling point. Reduce the heat, cover and simmer for 15 minutes. Serve with potatoes.

**Carroty beef:** Defrost and reheat a portion of mince curry. Meanwhile, finely chop 225 g/8 oz young carrots. Add to the curry with 225 g/8 oz finely diced potato. Meanwhile, boil 4 thick rings of peeled marrow or 4 large courgettes, halved lengthwise, until just tender. Drain sufficient of the cooking water into the curry to produce a very thick mixture suitable for stuffing the vegetables. Drain them, arrange in a greased shallow ovenproof dish and divide the curry mixture between the rings, or pile up in the courgette halves. Place under a hot grill for 5 minutes. (The crusty meat topping is delicious).

**Italian beef:** Shell and roughly chop 1 hard-boiled egg. Defrost a portion of mince curry and combine with a 396-g/14-oz can tomatoes and their liquid, the chopped egg and a few stuffed green olives. Reheat to boiling point then simmer for 5 minutes. Serve with buttered noodles.

# Lamb

## Gooseberry lamb

### Makes 8 portions

METRIC/IMPERIAL

| | |
|---|---|
| 2 teaspoons oil | I teaspoon dried and |
| 1·25 kg/2½ lb boneless lamb, cubed | ground rosemary |
| | salt and pepper |
| 2 large onions, sliced | I kg/2 lb potatoes, sliced |
| 350 g/12 oz gooseberries | 600 ml/I pint beef stock |
| I tablespoon brown sugar | |

1 Heat the oil and use to fry the lamb until browned on all sides. Add the onion and cook gently until beginning to soften. Add the gooseberries, sugar, rosemary and seasoning to taste, and stir well.
2 Arrange the lamb mixture and potato slices in a large ovenproof casserole and pour over the stock. Cover and cook in a moderate oven (160°C, 325°F, Gas Mark 3) for about 1½ hours, until the lamb is tender.
3 Divide the mixture between 2 boiling bags.
4 Reheat the frozen bag in boiling water for about 30 minutes.

**Variation:**

**Rhubarb lamb:** Substitute finely sliced rhubarb for the gooseberries and use chicken stock instead of beef stock.

## Cidered cutlet casserole

### Makes 8 portions

METRIC/IMPERIAL

| | |
|---|---|
| I tablespoon oil | 2 dessert apples, peeled |
| 16 small lamb cutlets | 50 g/2 oz seasoned flour |
| 25 g/I oz butter | 900 ml/I½ pints chicken |
| 225 g/8 oz small onions | stock |
| 6 sticks celery, sliced | 300 ml/½ pint dry cider |
| 225 g/8 oz button mushrooms | salt and pepper |
| I large cooking apple, peeled | |

1 Heat the oil and use to fry the cutlets gently on both sides until golden brown. Transfer them to a large ovenproof casserole.
2 Add the butter to the juices in the pan and use to fry the onions and celery gently for 5 minutes. Add these to the cutlets with the mushrooms. Core and slice all the apples and place in the casserole.
3 Sprinkle the flour into the juices remaining in the pan and stir well. Gradually add the stock and cider and bring to the boil, stirring constantly. Season to taste, pour over the cutlet mixture and stir well.
4 Cover and cook in a moderate oven (180°C, 350°F, Gas Mark 4) for about 1 hour, until the cutlets are tender.
5 Divide between 2 ovenproof dishes or foil containers for freezing.
6 Defrost before reheating in a moderately hot oven (190°C, 375°F, Gas Mark 5) for about 40 minutes, stirring occasionally.

# Turkish lamb with apricots

**Makes 8 portions**

METRIC/IMPERIAL

| | |
|---|---|
| 1·25 kg/2½ lb boneless lean lamb | 1 teaspoon dried sage |
| 4 large tomatoes, peeled | 1 teaspoon dried dill |
| 1 large green pepper, deseeded | 1 teaspoon ground bay leaves |
| 4 large onions, sliced | 1 tablespoon tomato purée |
| 100 g/4 oz dried apricots, chopped | generous 1 litre/2 pints chicken stock |
| 2 cloves garlic, crushed | salt and pepper |

1 Cut the lamb into neat cubes and place in a large saucepan. Slice the tomatoes and the green pepper and add to the pan with the onion, apricot, garlic, herbs and spice.
2 Stir the tomato purée into the stock and season to taste. Pour over the lamb mixture and bring to the boil. Cover and simmer for about 1½ hours, until the lamb is tender. Adjust seasoning if necessary.
3 Freeze in 2 boiling bags.
4 Reheat frozen bags in boiling water for about 30 minutes. Serve with fluffy boiled rice.

## Variations:

**Lamb bolognaise:** Omit the apricots and mince the lamb. Reduce the cooking time to 1 hour. Thicken with 2 tablespoons moistened cornflour before freezing. Serve with spaghetti or noodles.

**Pork and prune hot pot:** Substitute bladebone of pork for the lamb and 225 g/8 oz dried prunes for the apricots. Omit the tomatoes and tomato purée.

# Noisettes with cucumber sauce

**Makes 8 portions**

METRIC/IMPERIAL

| | |
|---|---|
| 16 lamb cutlets, boned | 6 tablespoons orange juice |
| 2 tablespoons oil | 1 chicken stock cube |
| 25 g/1 oz butter | 150 ml/¼ pint boiling water |
| 1 medium cucumber, peeled | salt and pepper |
| 2 teaspoons finely grated orange zest | 1 bunch watercress |
| | 1 tablespoon cornflour |

1 Tie the cutlets with string to make each one a neat round noisette. Heat the oil and butter and use to brown the noisettes on each side.
2 Coarsely grate the cucumber and add to the pan with the orange zest and juice. Dissolve the stock cube in the water and add to the pan with seasoning to taste.
3 Cover and cook gently for about 45 minutes, until the meat is tender. Arrange the noisettes in two foil containers.
4 Strip the watercress leaves from the stalks and chop them finely. Add to the cucumber mixture with the cornflour moistened with cold water. Bring to the boil, stirring constantly. Cook for 2 minutes and adjust the seasoning if necessary.

5 Pour the sauce over the noisettes before freezing.
6 Defrost and then reheat in a moderately hot oven (190°C, 375°F, Gas Mark 5) for about 30 minutes.

# Lamb with spring vegetables

**Makes 4–6 portions**

METRIC/IMPERIAL

| | |
|---|---|
| 1 kg/2¼ lb neck of lamb chops | 8 new carrots |
| 3 tablespoons seasoned flour | 8 silverskin pickled onions |
| 25 g/1 oz butter | 2 tablespoons clear honey |
| 1 tablespoon oil | 1 tablespoon mint jelly |
| 450 g/1 lb tiny new potatoes | 1 litre/1¾ pints chicken stock |
| | salt and pepper |

1 Coat the chops with seasoned flour. Heat the butter and oil and use to fry the chops until sealed on both sides. Transfer to an ovenproof casserole or foil container.
2 Scrub but do not peel the potatoes. Trim and scrape the carrots. Place these in the casserole with the pickled onions.
3 Sprinkle the rest of the seasoned flour into the juices in the pan and stir well. Add the honey, mint jelly and stock and bring to the boil, stirring constantly. Season to taste, pour over the meat mixture and stir well.
4 Cover and cook in a moderate oven (180°C, 350°F, Gas Mark 4) for 1½ hours, or until the lamb is tender.
5 Skim off any excess fat before freezing.
6 Defrost and then reheat in a moderately hot oven (190°C, 375°F, Gas Mark 5) for about 40 minutes.

# Corned lamb casserole

**Makes 8 portions**

METRIC/IMPERIAL

| | |
|---|---|
| 3 tablespoons oil | 600 ml/1 pint beef stock |
| 3 large onions, chopped | 1 teaspoon dried and ground rosemary |
| 4 inner sticks celery, sliced | 2 tablespoons tomato ketchup |
| 196-g/7½-oz can sweet corn kernels | salt and pepper |
| 8 large lamb chump chops | 225-g/8-oz can baked beans in tomato sauce |
| 4 tablespoons well-seasoned flour | |

1 Heat the oil and use to fry the onion and celery until pale golden and beginning to soften. Transfer to a large ovenproof casserole with the sweet corn and liquid from the can.
2 Coat the chops with seasoned flour, add to the pan and fry until golden brown on both sides. Add these to the casserole.
3 Stir any remaining seasoned flour into the juices in the pan. Gradually add the stock and bring to the boil, stirring constantly. Add the rosemary and ketchup and season to taste. Pour over the lamb mixture.

**4** Cook in a moderate oven (180°C, 350°F, Gas Mark 4) for 2 hours, or until the lamb is tender. Stir in the beans and sauce from the can.

**5** Arrange the chops in two foil containers and pour the sauce over before freezing.

**6** Defrost and then reheat in a moderately hot oven (190°C, 375°F, Gas Mark 5) for about 35 minutes.

## Kowloon lamb

**Makes 8 portions**

METRIC/IMPERIAL

2 lean breasts of lamb, boned
1 large onion, sliced
225-g/8-oz can bamboo shoots
225-g/8-oz can pineapple pieces

150 ml/¼ pint white vinegar
150 ml/¼ pint chicken stock
3 tablespoons brown sugar
1 teaspoon salt
2 tablespoons arrowroot

**1** Trim and cut each breast into 8 strips. Fry the strips in their own fat until crisp and golden brown on all sides. Drain and transfer to an ovenproof casserole with the onion. Drain the bamboo shoot, slice and add to the casserole with the drained pineapple pieces.

**2** Mix together the liquid from the can of bamboo shoot, the pineapple syrup, vinegar, stock, sugar and salt. Stir well and pour over the lamb mixture.

**3** Cook in a moderate oven (180°C, 350°F, Gas Mark 4) for about 1¼ hours, until the lamb is tender. Moisten the arrowroot with a little cold water, stir into the casserole until well blended and return to the oven for a further 10 minutes.

**4** Check the seasoning before freezing in 2 boiling bags.

**5** Reheat frozen bag in a pan of boiling water for about 30 minutes. Serve with fluffy boiled rice.

# Pork

## Mild pork goulash

METRIC/IMPERIAL

4 tablespoons oil
1·25 kg/2½ lb bladebone of pork, cubed
4 large onions, chopped
2 cloves garlic, chopped
1 tablespoon sweet paprika pepper

450 g/1 lb tomatoes, peeled
100 g/4 oz tomato purée
150 ml/¼ pint water
salt and pepper
150 ml/¼ pint natural yogurt

**1** Heat the oil and use to brown the meat all over. Add the onions and garlic and cook for 3 minutes. Sprinkle in the paprika and stir well.

**2** Chop the tomatoes, add to the pan with the tomato purée and water. Season to taste, bring to the boil, cover and simmer for about 2 hours, until the meat is tender.

**3** Adjust the seasoning and stir in the yogurt.

**4** Reheat and serve with buttered noodles.

**Variation:**

**Spicy pork goulash:** Use hot paprika pepper to suit your taste instead of sweet paprika, and if liked, add a dash of cayenne and Tabasco sauce.

## Pork and sausage cassoulet

**Makes 8 portions**

METRIC/IMPERIAL

225 g/8 oz haricot beans
100 g/4 oz piece streaky bacon, derinded
2 cloves garlic, crushed
2 tablespoons chopped parsley
¼ teaspoon ground bay leaves
pinch of dried sage

*when serving:*
25 g/1 oz butter

2 large onions, sliced
0·5 kg/1¼ lb cooked pork, diced
225 g/8 oz frankfurters, sliced
3 tablespoons tomato purée
salt and pepper

**1** Soak the beans in cold water to cover overnight then drain.

**2** Dice the bacon and place in a saucepan with the drained beans, garlic, parsley, ground bay leaves, sage and onion. Pour in water just to cover and boil gently for about 1½ hours, until the beans are tender.

**3** Drain the beans mixture and boil the cooking liquid until reduced to 450 ml/¾ pint.

**4** Put the pork, frankfurters and bean mixture into a large ovenproof casserole. Dissolve the tomato purée in the reduced stock and season well. Pour over the pork mixture, cover and cook in a cool oven (150°C, 300°F, Gas Mark 2) for 1¼ hours. Add a little water if necessary to prevent the cassoulet drying out.

**5** Divide the mixture between 2 foil containers.

**6** Defrost, uncover and dot with butter. Reheat in a moderate oven (190°C, 350°F, Gas Mark 4) for about 45 minutes.

# Rhubarb and ginger chops

**Makes 4 portions**

METRIC/IMPERIAL
2 tablespoons oil
4 large pork chops
I large onion, chopped
225 g/8 oz rhubarb,
  sliced
¼ teaspoon ground ginger
I piece preserved ginger,
  chopped

I tablespoon ginger syrup
  from jar
150 ml/¼ pint chicken
  stock
salt and pepper
2 teaspoons cornflour

1 Heat the oil and use to fry the chops until golden brown on both sides. Remove from the pan and keep warm.
2 Add the onion to the juices remaining in the pan and fry gently until soft. Add the rhubarb, ground ginger, chopped ginger, ginger syrup and stock and stir well.
3 Bring to the boil and arrange the chops on the mixture. Sprinkle with salt and pepper, cover and simmer for about 25 minutes, until the chops are tender.
4 Arrange the chops in a foil container. Moisten the cornflour with cold water, add to the pan and bring to the boil, stirring constantly, until thickened. Taste and adjust the seasoning if necessary.
5 Spoon the sauce over the chops before freezing.
6 Defrost and then reheat in a moderately hot oven (190°C, 375°F, Gas Mark 5) for about 30 minutes.


# Sausage and butterbean pot

**Makes 8 portions**

METRIC/IMPERIAL
4 tablespoons oil
I kg/2 lb beef sausages
4 large onions, sliced
225 g/8 oz mushrooms,
  sliced
425-g/15-oz can
  butterbeans, drained

600 ml/I pint brown ale
600 ml/I pint water
2 600-ml/I-pint packets
  onion soup powder
salt and pepper

1 Heat the oil and use to fry the sausages quickly until golden brown on all sides. Transfer to an ovenproof casserole.
2 Add the onion to the fat remaining in the pan and fry until golden brown. Add the mushrooms and fry for a further 2 minutes. Spoon the onion and mushrooms over the sausages with the butterbeans.
3 Pour the brown ale and water into the pan and whisk in the soup powder. Bring to the boil, stirring constantly, then season to taste and pour over the sausages.
4 Cover and cook in a moderate oven (180°C, 350°F, Gas Mark 4) for about 50 minutes.
5 Divide the mixture between 2 boiling bags before freezing.
6 Reheat the frozen bag in boiling water for about 30 minutes.


# Gammon with herby topping

**Makes 4 portions**

METRIC/IMPERIAL
2 tablespoons oil
4 100-g/4-oz gammon
  steaks
I large onion, chopped
25 g/I oz butter
6 tablespoons soft
  breadcrumbs

I teaspoon dried sage
½ teaspoon garlic salt
pepper
50 g/2 oz Cheddar cheese,
  grated

1 Heat the oil and use to fry the gammon steaks until just golden on both sides. Transfer them to a large foil container in a single layer.
2 Add the onion to the fat remaining in the pan and fry until golden brown. Stir in the butter, breadcrumbs, sage, garlic salt and a little pepper.
3 Sprinkle the breadcrumbs mixture over the gammon steaks and top with the cheese.
4 Cook in a moderate oven (180°C, 350°F, Gas Mark 4) for 30 minutes.
5 Cover with foil before freezing.
6 Place still frozen in a moderately hot oven (190°C, 375°F, Gas Mark 5) for 30 minutes, then remove the foil and return to the oven for a further 10–15 minutes, until heated through and the topping is crisp.

**Variation:**

**Herby topped pork:** Substitute 4 pork spare rib chops or shoulder steaks for the gammon steaks and cook for 45 minutes before freezing. Allow an additional 10–15 minutes for reheating before removing the foil.


# Pork chops in marmalade glaze

**Makes 4 portions**

METRIC/IMPERIAL
I orange
I tablespoon soy sauce
pinch of ground ginger

2 tablespoons orange jelly
  marmalade
4 pork spare-rib chops

1 Finely grate the rind from half the orange and squeeze the juice from the whole orange. Place both in a saucepan with the soy sauce, ginger and marmalade. Heat gently, stirring, until the mixture is smooth.
2 Trim the chops, place in a shallow polythene container and prick all over with a fork. Pour over the marmalade mixture and allow to stand for 2 hours, turning the chops once during this time.
3 Freeze in the liquid.
4 Defrost in the sealed container, then arrange the chops on a grid and cook under a moderately hot grill for about 20 minutes, turning occasionally and brushing with any remaining marmalade marinade. Serve with fluffy cooked rice.

**Variations:**

**Pork chops in tangerine glaze:** Substitute 3 tangerines for the orange and use the finely grated rind of one in the marinade.

**Pork chops in grapefruit glaze:** Substitute 1 ripe grapefruit for the orange and use the finely grated rind of slightly less than half in the marinade. Add 1 further tablespoon of marmalade if the mixture seems very tart.

**Pork chops in lemon marmalade glaze:** Substitute 1 lemon for the orange and use the finely grated rind of three-quarters of it in the marinade. Use lemon jelly marmalade instead of orange.

## Bacon and bean stew

### Makes 8 portions

METRIC/IMPERIAL

225 g/8 oz haricot beans
1·5 kg/3 lb piece of
   collar bacon or slipper
   bacon
75 g/3 oz butter
3 large onions, chopped

4 tablespoons flour
900 ml/1½ pints chicken
   stock
450 g/1 lb carrots, sliced
pepper

1 Soak the beans in cold water to cover overnight. Drain well.
2 Derind the bacon and cut the meat into large dice. Cover with cold water, bring to the boil, then drain very well.
3 Melt the butter in a large saucepan and use to fry the onion gently until soft. Sprinkle in the flour and stir well. Gradually add the stock and bring to the boil, stirring constantly. Add the soaked beans, carrot and bacon and bring back to the boil.
4 Cover and simmer for about 1½ hours, until the bacon and beans are both tender. Add pepper to taste.
5 Divide the mixture between 2 boiling bags before freezing.
6 Reheat the frozen bag in boiling water for about 30 minutes.

### Variation:

**Bacon and leek stew:** Substitute 4 large sliced leeks for the onions and use a drained 425-g/15-oz can of butterbeans instead of the haricot beans. Add these for the last 15 minutes of cooking time.

# Offal

## Pigs' liver in spicy sauce

METRIC/IMPERIAL

1 kg/2 lb pigs' liver
150 ml/¼ pint milk
100 g/4 oz dripping or
   lard
450 g/1 lb onions,
   chopped
100 g/4 oz flour
2 beef stock cubes
generous 1 litre/2 pints
   water

225-g/8-oz can tomatoes,
   chopped
1 teaspoon brown sugar
1 teaspoon dried mixed
   herbs
few drops Tabasco or chilli
   sauce
salt and pepper

1 Cut the liver into thin strips. Place in a bowl and pour over the milk. Allow to stand for about 45 minutes.
2 Melt the fat and use to fry the onion gently until pale golden. Stir in the flour and cook for 3 minutes.
3 Add the crumbled stock cubes, water, chopped tomatoes and their liquid, the sugar, herbs and seasonings. Bring to the boil, stirring constantly. Cover and simmer for 3–4 minutes.
4 Drain the liver strips, add to the sauce and stir well. Cover and simmer for 10 minutes. Stir in sufficient of the milk used for soaking the liver to make a smooth thick sauce.

### Variations:

**Orchard liver:** Peel, core and thinly slice a medium cooking apple. Add to the pan with the liver strips. Adjust seasoning at the end of cooking time.

**Curried liver strips:** Add 50 g/2 oz seedless raisins with the sliced onion. Omit the sugar and combine 1 teaspoon curry powder with the flour.

**Liver with apricots:** Add 50 g/2 oz dried apricot halves with the onion. Omit the sugar and add 1 tablespoon redcurrant jelly with the water.

## Lambs' tongues in piquant sauce

### Makes 8 portions

METRIC/IMPERIAL

8 lambs' tongues
2 chicken stock cubes
900 ml/1½ pints water
1 large onion, chopped
½ teaspoon ground cloves
1 teaspoon ground mace

3 bay leaves
salt and pepper
25 g/1 oz butter
25 g/1 oz flour
50 g/2 oz pickled
   gherkins, sliced

1 Soak and scrub the tongues well. Place in a large saucepan with the stock cubes, water, onion, spices, bay leaves and seasoning to taste. Bring to the boil, skim, cover and simmer for 2 hours, or until the tongues are tender. Discard the bay leaves.
2 Remove the tongues, skin and trim off the roots. Keep warm.

**3** Melt the fat, stir in the flour and cook for 1 minute. Gradually add the cooking stock and bring to the boil, stirring constantly, until smooth. Add the gherkins and continue cooking until the sauce reaches boiling point and becomes thick. Taste and adjust the seasoning.

**4** Slice the tongues and add to the sauce.

**Variations:**

Lambs' tongues in caper sauce: Substitute 2 tablespoons drained capers for the gherkins and season carefully.

Lambs' tongues in cranberry sauce: Substitute a 175-g/6-oz jar of cranberry sauce for the gherkins and stir well until it has completely blended into the sauce. Use black pepper for seasoning.

## Spiced kidney and carrot stew

**Makes 8 portions**

METRIC/IMPERIAL

| | |
|---|---|
| 1 kg/2 lb ox kidney | 2 tablespoons tomato |
| 50 g/2 oz seasoned flour | ketchup |
| 6 tablespoons oil | 900 ml/1½ pints beef |
| 2 cloves garlic, crushed | stock |
| 1 tablespoon curry | 0·75 kg/1½ lb carrots, |
| powder | sliced |
| ½ teaspoon mild chilli | salt |
| powder | |

**1** Trim the kidney and cut into small pieces. Coat with seasoned flour. Heat the oil in a saucepan and use to fry the kidney until brown on all sides. Remove from the pan and keep warm.

**2** Add the garlic to the fat remaining in the pan and stir in the curry powder, chilli powder and ketchup. Cook, stirring all the time, for 5 minutes. Sprinkle in any remaining seasoned flour and gradually add the stock. Bring to the boil, stirring constantly.

**3** Return the kidney to the pan with the carrots, stir well and bring back to the boil. Cover and simmer for about 1¼ hours, until the kidney is tender. Add salt to taste.

**4** Divide the mixture between 2 boiling bags before freezing.

**5** Reheat the frozen bag in boiling water for about 30 minutes.

## Liver and bacon casserole

**Makes 8 portions**

METRIC/IMPERIAL

| | |
|---|---|
| 100 g/4 oz dripping | 175 g/6 oz streaky bacon, |
| 2 large onions, sliced | derinded |
| 0·75 kg/1¾ lb ox liver | 600 ml/1 pint beef stock |
| 50 g/2 oz seasoned flour | ¼ teaspoon ground nutmeg |
| | salt and pepper |

**1** Melt the dripping and use to fry the onion until golden brown.

**2** Meanwhile, trim and thinly slice the liver. Coat with seasoned flour, add to the pan and fry until golden brown on both sides. Add the bacon rashers and fry for a further 3 minutes. Transfer to an ovenproof casserole.

**3** Sprinkle any remaining seasoned flour into the juices left in the pan and stir well. Gradually add the stock and bring to the boil, stirring constantly. Add the nutmeg and season to taste. Pour over the liver mixture.

**4** Cover and cook in a moderate oven (160°C, 325°F, Gas Mark 3) for about 1½ hours, until the liver is tender.

**5** Divide the mixture between 2 ovenproof or foil containers before freezing.

**6** Defrost, uncover and then reheat in a moderately hot oven (190°C, 375°F, Gas Mark 5) for about 45 minutes.

**Variation:**

Cidered liver and bacon casserole: Substitute 600 ml/1 pint dry cider and a beef stock cube for the beef stock. Peel, core and slice 2 dessert apples and add to the liver mixture before freezing.

## Stuffed hearts with vegetables

**Makes 8 portions**

METRIC/IMPERIAL

| | |
|---|---|
| 2 large onions | 8 lambs' hearts |
| 100 g/4 oz butter | 1 medium swede, diced |
| 100-g/4-oz packet parsley | 4 large leeks, sliced |
| and thyme stuffing mix | 50 g/2 oz flour |
| 2 teaspoons | 600 ml/1 pint beef stock |
| Worcestershire sauce | salt and pepper |
| 2 tablespoons chopped | |
| parsley | |

**1** Grate 1 onion and fry gently in half the butter for 3 minutes. Stir in the dry stuffing mix, Worcestershire sauce and parsley and add sufficient boiling water to make a firm stuffing.

**2** Trim the hearts, stuff them and tie with white string.

**3** Slice the remaining onion and fry in the rest of the butter with the swede and leek until beginning to soften. Sprinkle in the flour and stir well. Gradually add the stock and bring to the boil, stirring constantly. Season to taste and spoon into a large ovenproof casserole.

**4** Stand the stuffed hearts in the braise, cover and cook in a moderate oven (180°C, 350°F, Gas Mark 4) for 1½ hours, or until the hearts are tender.

**5** Pack the hearts in two foil containers and pour the braise over them before freezing.

**6** Defrost and then reheat in a moderately hot oven (190°C, 375°F, Gas Mark 5) for about 30 minutes.

## Summertime liver

### Makes 8 portions

METRIC/IMPERIAL

| | |
|---|---|
| 1 kg/2 lb lambs' liver, sliced | 4 large tomatoes, peeled |
| 50 g/2 oz seasoned flour | 1 medium cucumber, peeled |
| 50 g/2 oz butter | 1 teaspoon dried mixed herbs or 2 tablespoons chopped fresh herbs |
| 3 tablespoons oil | |
| 1 red pepper, deseeded | |
| 1 green pepper, deseeded | 450 ml/¾ pint beef stock |
| 1 large onion, chopped | salt and pepper |

1 Coat the liver in seasoned flour. Heat the butter and oil in a saucepan and use to fry the liver until brown on both sides. Remove from the pan and keep warm.
2 Slice the peppers and add to the pan with the onion. Fry gently until beginning to soften. Slice the tomatoes and cucumber and add to the onion mixture with the herbs. Cover and cook gently for 10 minutes.
3 Sprinkle in any remaining seasoned flour and gradually add the stock. Bring to the boil, stirring constantly.
4 Season to taste and return the liver to the pan. Stir well, cover and simmer for about 25 minutes, until the liver is just tender.
5 Divide the mixture between 2 boiling bags before freezing.
6 Reheat the frozen bag in boiling water for about 30 minutes.

## Creamed tripe and onions

### Makes 4 portions

METRIC/IMPERIAL

| | |
|---|---|
| 0·5 kg/1¼ lb tripe | 4 teaspoons cornflour |
| 3 large onions, sliced | 300 ml/½ pint milk |
| 450 ml/¾ pint chicken stock | 150 ml/¼ pint soured cream |
| salt and pepper | |

1 Cut the tripe into neat squares and place in a saucepan. Cover with cold water, bring to the boil then drain.
2 Add the onion to the tripe, pour over the stock and season to taste. Cover and simmer for about 1½ hours, until the tripe is tender.
3 Moisten the cornflour with a little of the milk and add to the tripe mixture with the remaining milk. Bring to the boil, stirring constantly, until thickened. Cook for 2 minutes then stir in the cream and adjust the seasoning if necessary.
4 Freeze in a polythene container.
5 Defrost and then reheat in a saucepan, stirring frequently.

# Meat marinades

## Red wine and garlic marinade

### Makes about 300 ml/½ pint

METRIC/IMPERIAL

| | |
|---|---|
| 3 cloves garlic | 6 tablespoons robust red wine |
| 1 medium onion, chopped | |
| 2 sticks celery, chopped | 150 ml/¼ pint olive oil or corn oil |
| ¼ teaspoon dry mustard | |
| 3 tablespoons lemon juice | salt and pepper |

Finely chop the garlic, onion, and celery. Mix together the mustard and lemon juice and gradually whisk in the wine and oil. Stir in the prepared vegetables and season ready to use.

## Lemon herb marinade

### Makes about 300 ml/½ pint

METRIC/IMPERIAL

| | |
|---|---|
| 4 spring onions, chopped | 75 ml/3 fl oz lemon juice |
| 3 teaspoons dried mixed herbs | 150 ml/¼ pint olive or corn oil |
| ¼ teaspoon Tabasco sauce | salt and pepper |
| finely grated rind of 1 lemon | |

Place the onion, herbs, Tabasco and lemon rind in a bowl and whisk in the lemon juice and oil. Season to taste and allow to stand for 2 hours before using.

## Sweet fruity marinade

### Makes about 600 ml/1 pint

METRIC/IMPERIAL

| | |
|---|---|
| 450 ml/¾ pint pineapple juice | 2 tablespoons clear honey |
| 1 tablespoon olive or corn oil | 4 tablespoons tomato ketchup |
| 1 tablespoon French mustard | pinch of cayenne pepper |
| | salt and pepper |

Place all the ingredients together in a small saucepan with seasoning to taste. Bring to the boil, stirring constantly. Boil gently until reduced to 300 ml/½ pint. Use when cold.

## Ginger marinade

### Makes about 300 ml/½ pint

METRIC/IMPERIAL

| | |
|---|---|
| 1 tablespoon corn oil | 2 tablespoons soft brown sugar |
| 150 ml/¼ pint orange juice | 1 teaspoon ground ginger |
| 1 tablespoon lemon juice | 2 teaspoons prepared mustard |
| 3 tablespoons tomato purée | 1 teaspoon salt |

Place all the ingredients in a saucepan and bring to the boil, stirring constantly. Simmer for 3 minutes. Use when cold.

# Cooked meat and soya

## Hasty chicken curry

**Makes 4 portions**

METRIC/IMPERIAL

| | |
|---|---|
| 50 g/2 oz butter | 1 tablespoon curry |
| 2 tablespoons oil | powder |
| 1 clove garlic, crushed | 600 ml/1 pint chicken |
| 1 large onion, sliced | stock |
| 100 g/4 oz potato, diced | 350 g/12 oz cooked |
| 100 g/4 oz carrot, | chicken, diced |
| chopped | 25 g/1 oz sultanas |
| 3 tablespoons flour | salt |

1 Heat the butter and oil and use to fry the garlic, onion, potato and carrot until soft and golden brown.
2 Sprinkle in the flour and curry powder, then gradually add the stock and bring to the boil, stirring constantly. Fold in the chicken, sultanas and a little salt, cover and simmer for about 30 minutes. Adjust the seasoning if necessary.
3 Freeze in a boiling bag.
4 Reheat the frozen bag in boiling water for about 30 minutes. Serve with fluffy boiled rice, mango chutney, cucumber slices in natural yogurt or banana slices sprinkled with salted peanuts.

### Hint:

The curry can be made with cooked lamb, pork or beef, according to what you have left over. This is a fairly mild curry so adjust the amount of curry powder if you like your curry with a stronger flavour.

## Monday lamb in paprika sauce

**Makes 4 portions**

METRIC/IMPERIAL

| | |
|---|---|
| 50 g/2 oz butter | 150 ml/¼ pint soured |
| 100 g/4 oz button | cream |
| mushrooms, sliced | 1 tablespoon sweet |
| 350–450 g/12 oz–1 lb | paprika pepper |
| cooked lean lamb, | 1 tablespoon cornflour |
| sliced | salt and pepper |

1 Melt the butter and use to fry the mushrooms until golden brown. Drain and arrange these in an oven-proof dish or foil container with the slices of meat.
2 Add the soured cream to the fat remaining in the pan with the paprika, and heat gently. Moisten the cornflour with a little cold water, add to the pan and bring to the boil, stirring constantly, until the sauce thickens. Simmer for 2 minutes and season to taste.
3 Spoon the sauce over the meat and mushrooms before freezing.
4 Defrost and then reheat in a moderate oven (180°C, 350°F, Gas Mark 4) for about 40 minutes.

### Variation:

**Beef in cream sauce:** Substitute slices of cooked beef for the lamb and use single cream instead of soured cream. Season with onion salt and pepper.

## Half and half casserole curry

**Makes 8 portions**

METRIC/IMPERIAL

| | |
|---|---|
| 50 g/2 oz dripping | 2 tablespoons flour |
| 1 large onion, chopped | 300 ml/½ pint beef stock |
| 225 g/8 oz swede or | 75 g/3 oz seedless raisins |
| turnip, diced | 425-g/15-oz can soya |
| 450 g/1 lb minced beef | mince in gravy |
| 1 tablespoon curry | salt |
| powder | |

1 Melt the dripping and use to fry the onion and swede or turnip gently until beginning to soften.
2 Add the minced beef and fry briskly, stirring, until the meat changes colour and looks crumbly.
3 Sprinkle over the curry powder and flour and stir well. Cook for 3 minutes, stirring constantly. Add the stock and bring to the boil, stirring all the time. Add the raisins and the contents of the can of soya mince in gravy.
4 Bring to the boil, cover and simmer for 20 minutes. Taste and add salt if necessary.
5 Divide the mixture between 2 boiling bags for freezing.
6 Reheat the frozen bag in boiling water for about 30 minutes.

### Variations:

**Date and apple soya curry:** Substitute 2 peeled, cored and sliced cooking apples for the swede and 75 g/3 oz chopped, stoned dates for the raisins.

**Soya chunk curry:** Use 2 425-g/15-oz cans of soya casserole chunks instead of the soya mince and minced beef. Reduce the stock to 150 ml/¼ pint.

## Pork with peanut potato balls

**Makes 8 portions**

METRIC/IMPERIAL

| | |
|---|---|
| 450 g/1 lb cooked carrots | salt and pepper |
| 350–450 g/12 oz–1 lb | 1 egg, beaten |
| cooked pork, chopped | 175 g/6 oz salted peanuts, |
| 1 kg/2 lb potatoes | chopped |
| 4 egg yolks, beaten | oil for frying |
| ½ teaspoon ground nutmeg | |

1 Finely chop the carrots and mix with the pork. Divide the mixture between two shallow shaped foil containers and spread smoothly.
2 Slice the potatoes and cook in boiling salted water until tender. Drain well then return the open pan to gentle heat to dry the potato as much as possible. Mash, and beat in the egg yolks, nutmeg and seasoning to taste. Chill until firm.
3 Divide the mixture into 16 equal portions and shape each into a round ball. Dip the balls in the beaten egg and coat all over with salted peanuts.
4 Deep fry, a few at a time, in hot oil for 3 minutes, or until golden all over. Drain well on absorbent paper.

**5** Place 8 balls in each container and press down lightly into the meat mixture. Cover to freeze.

**6** Uncover and reheat from frozen in a moderately hot oven (200°C, 400°F, Gas Mark 6) for about 25 minutes.

## Michaelmas beef

### Makes 8 portions

METRIC/IMPERIAL
200 ml/6 fl oz water
2 60-g/20-oz packets soya meat extender
0·75 kg/1½ lb minced beef
1 medium cucumber, diced
1 large onion, chopped
2 tablespoons oil
2 tablespoons vinegar
2 teaspoons soft brown sugar
1 teaspoon dried mixed herbs
salt and pepper
450 g/1 lb tomatoes

**1** Add water to the soya meat extender as instructed on the packets and combine this mixture with the minced beef.

**2** Fry the cucumber and onion in the oil in a large frying pan for 3 minutes. Add the meat mixture, vinegar, sugar, herbs and seasoning to taste. Cook gently for 10 minutes, stirring frequently.

**3** Roughly chop the tomatoes, add to the pan, cover and simmer for 15 minutes. Adjust the seasoning.

**4** Divide between 2 boiling bags for freezing.

**5** Reheat the frozen bag in boiling water for about 30 minutes.

# Meat kebabs

## Basic marinated meat kebabs

### Makes 4 portions

METRIC/IMPERIAL
450 g/1 lb lean tender meat (lamb, pork or beef)
150 ml/¼ pint marinade (see below)

*when serving:*
button mushrooms
bay leaves
squares of green or red pepper
silverskin pickled onions
tiny whole tomatoes
pineapple cubes
chunks of cooked beetroot
chunks of cucumber
wedges of fresh apple brushed with oil

**1** Cut the meat carefully into fairly large cubes of a size suitable to thread on a skewer (2·5 cm/1 inch).

**2** Place the meat in a polythene container, pour over the marinade of your choice, cover and refrigerate for 24 hours before freezing.

**3** Defrost and then allow sufficient of the other ingredients to alternate single items with cubes of meat on each skewer. Thread the skewers then brush the loaded skewers well with remaining marinade. Place under a hot grill for 6–8 minutes, turning the skewers frequently and brushing with the marinade, until cooked through.

# Quick-service light meals

In these busy days a meal for one member of the family may be required almost at a moment's notice, as often as the conventional meal for four. Many of these dishes are specially adapted to be frozen in individual portions, or so planned that you can easily remove one serving. For example, single pizzas, sandwich toasting slices, patties and croquettes.

### Plate meals
Few housewives cook specially to produce plate meals, but many prepare extra quantities when cooking an everyday meal to provide sufficient leftovers to fill one or two plates for the freezer. This is particularly useful to bear in mind when you are cooking a joint, a large chicken, or a turkey at the weekend. If you have not a large supply of plates to spare, foil trays with dimpled divisions are ideal, or even (for small snack meals) foil flan cases. A few slices of meat masked with gravy should fill one third of the dish, cooked potato, rice or pasta topped with a nut of butter a second third, and the remaining space filled with a cooked vegetable. Cool and cover with foil. Label very carefully as it would be a pity to reheat a meal and find that, for example, the vegetable is not liked by the person for whom it was intended. Reheating instructions should be given on the label as well so that even the uninitiated can choose and prepare a plate dinner successfully.

### Useful extenders
Some snack meals can quickly be converted into main meals by serving together with additions such as instant mashed potato or small pasta shapes which cook in a few minutes. Extra quickly-cooked frozen vegetables, fried mushrooms and tomatoes in the form of a salad are other extenders you are likely to have on hand.

# Pizzas

## Basic onion pizza

### Makes 1 pizza, 2 portions

METRIC/IMPERIAL

| | |
|---|---|
| 225 g/8 oz risen white bread dough (see page 11) | 1 canned red pimento, chopped |
| 50 g/2 oz butter | garlic salt and pepper |
| 225 g/8 oz onion, sliced | 50 g/2 oz Mozzarella cheese, sliced |

1 Roll out the bread dough to make a 20-cm/8-inch round and place on a greased baking sheet.
2 Melt the butter and use to fry the onion gently until soft. Stir in the pimento and season to taste with garlic salt and pepper. Spoon the onion mixture over the pizza base and cover with the cheese. Allow to rise until double in bulk.
3 Bake in a moderately hot oven (190°C, 375°F, Gas Mark 5) for 30 minutes.
4 Open freeze before packing.
5 Defrost and then uncover, place on a baking sheet and reheat in a hot oven (220°C, 425°F, Gas Mark 7) for 10 minutes.

### Variation:

**Sweet apple and spice pizza:** Make the bread base as above and top with 225 g/8 oz prepared cooking apple slices. Melt 15 g/½ oz butter with 2 tablespoons lemon juice and use to brush the apple slices. Mix 2 tablespoons soft brown sugar with 1 teaspoon ground cinnamon and sprinkle over the top.

## Mini pizzas

### Makes 4 mini pizzas, 4 portions

METRIC/IMPERIAL

| | |
|---|---|
| 450 g/1 lb risen white bread dough (see page 11) | 1 tablespoon drained capers |
| 1 tablespoon oil | 1 tablespoon Parmesan cheese, grated |
| 200-g/7-oz can mackerel in tomato sauce | |

1 Divide the dough into 4 equal portions and roll out each one to a 10-cm/4-inch round. Place on greased baking sheets.
2 Bone and flake the mackerel and divide among the 4 pizza bases. Spread evenly. Scatter a few capers on each one and sprinkle with a little cheese. Allow to rise until double in size.
3 Bake in a moderately hot oven (190°C, 375°F, Gas Mark 5) for about 25 minutes.
4 Open freeze before packing.
5 Arrange on baking sheets and reheat from frozen in a hot oven (220°C, 425°F, Gas Mark 7) for about 15 minutes.

## Bap pizzas

### Makes 12 pizzas, 6 portions

METRIC/IMPERIAL

| | |
|---|---|
| 6 baps | 175 g/6 oz Gouda cheese, grated |
| 50 g/2 oz butter | 1 teaspoon dried oregano |
| 225 g/8 oz tomatoes, peeled | 24 stoned black olives |
| salt and pepper | 50 g/2 oz anchovy fillets |

1 Split and butter the baps. Slice the tomatoes and arrange on the bap halves. Season with salt and pepper.
2 Mix together the cheese and oregano and sprinkle liberally over the tomato slices.
3 Decorate each bap pizza with pieces of olive and anchovy fillets. Drizzle over the oil from the can.
4 Open freeze before packing.
5 Unwrap and grill from frozen until heated through and the topping is golden brown.

## Quick tomato pizza

### Makes 2 pizzas – 4 portions

METRIC/IMPERIAL

*base:*

| | |
|---|---|
| 225 g/8 oz plain flour | 2 tablespoons corn oil |
| 2 teaspoons baking powder | 125 ml/4 fl oz water |
| | oil for frying |

*filling:*

| | |
|---|---|
| 6 medium tomatoes, sliced | 100 g/4 oz garlic sausage, sliced |
| 1 teaspoon Aromat seasoning | few stoned olives |
| | 225 g/8 oz Gouda cheese, grated |

1 Mix together the flour, baking powder, oil and water to form a dough. Divide into two and roll out each piece to a 17·5-cm/7-inch circle.
2 Heat a little oil in a large frying pan, add one pizza base and fry over a moderate heat until golden brown, turn over and fry the other side until brown. Slide on to a baking tray and fry the other base in the same way.
3 Arrange the tomato slices on the pizzas and season with Aromat. Cover with the slices of sausage, the olives and grated cheese.
4 Freeze before cooking.
5 Arrange on baking sheets and bake from frozen in a moderately hot oven (200°C, 400°F, Gas Mark 6) for 30 minutes.

### Variation:

**Quick courgette pizza:** Substitute 225 g/8 oz sliced courgettes for the tomatoes. Blanch by plunging into a pan of boiling water for 1 minute. Drain well. Use 8 medium derinded rashers of streaky bacon instead of the garlic sausage.

# Pasta

## Neptune noodles

### Makes 4 portions

METRIC/IMPERIAL

| | |
|---|---|
| 2 small red peppers, deseeded | $\frac{1}{4}$ teaspoon dried basil |
| 50-g/2-oz can anchovy fillets | $\frac{1}{2}$ teaspoon dried tarragon |
| I large onion, chopped | 4 cod fillets or steaks, cubed |
| I clove garlic, crushed | black pepper |
| 2 tablespoons oil | 225 g/8 oz tagliatelle |
| 450 ml/$\frac{3}{4}$ pint tomato juice | |

1 Chop the peppers and anchovy fillets and cook gently with the onion and garlic in the oil (including the oil from the can), until all the vegetables are soft. Stir in the tomato juice, herbs and fish. Season with pepper to taste.
2 Simmer until the fish is just tender. Meanwhile, cook the tagliatelle in boiling salted water until tender. Drain well and toss with the fish sauce.
3 Pack in a boiling bag.
4 Reheat frozen bag in boiling water for about 30 minutes.

## Macaroni kedgeree

### Makes 4 portions

METRIC/IMPERIAL

| | |
|---|---|
| 225 g/8 oz quick cook macaroni | 4 hard-boiled eggs, chopped |
| 225 g/8 oz boil-in-the-bag smoked cod or haddock fillet | I tablespoon chopped parsley |
| 50 g/2 oz butter | rind of I lemon, grated |
| | salt and pepper |

1 Cook the macaroni in boiling salted water until tender. Drain well.
2 Meanwhile, cook the fish. Reserve the liquid, remove any skin and bone and flake the fish.
3 Melt the butter, add the macaroni, fish, chopped egg, parsley and lemon rind and mix well. Stir in the reserved fish liquid, and season to taste.
4 Pack in a boiling bag.
5 Reheat the frozen bag in boiling water for about 30 minutes.

## Macaroni and cheese fritters

### Makes 4 portions

METRIC/IMPERIAL

| | |
|---|---|
| 50 g/2 oz quick cook macaroni | salt and pepper |
| 3 eggs | 8 rashers streaky bacon, derinded |
| 100 g/4 oz cheese, grated | oil for frying |
| I teaspoon prepared mustard | |

1 Cook the macaroni in boiling salted water until tender. Drain well.
2 Beat the eggs with the cheese, mustard and seasoning to taste. Fold in the macaroni.
3 Roughly chop the bacon and fry until crisp. Add to the macaroni mixture.
4 Heat the oil and use to fry tablespoons of the macaroni mixture until golden brown all over.
5 Drain very well on absorbent paper before freezing.
6 Arrange the fritters on a baking sheet and reheat from frozen in a moderately hot oven (200°C, 400°F, Gas Mark 6) for about 15 minutes.

### Hint:

If wished, arrange some halved tomatoes, dotted with butter, on the baking sheet with the frozen fritters and these will cook while the fritters are reheating.

## Sausage lasagne rolls

### Makes 4 portions

METRIC/IMPERIAL

| | |
|---|---|
| 450 g/I lb large pork sausages | 2 tablespoons tomato purée |
| 8 sheets lasagne verdi | I teaspoon sugar |
| 25 g/I oz butter | 2 tablespoons chopped parsley |
| 25 g/I oz flour | salt and pepper |
| 150 ml/$\frac{1}{4}$ pint water | 25 g/I oz Cheddar cheese, grated |
| 397-g/14-oz can tomatoes | |
| I teaspoon Worcestershire sauce | |

1 Grill or fry the sausages for about 10 minutes until golden brown all over and cooked through.
2 Meanwhile, lower the lasagne into boiling salted water and simmer for about 10 minutes, until just tender. Drain well.
3 At the same time, melt the butter in a saucepan and stir in the flour. Cook for 1 minute, gradually add the water, tomatoes and their liquid and the Worcestershire sauce and bring to the boil, stirring constantly. Stir in the tomato purée, sugar, parsley and seasoning to taste.
4 Wrap each cooked sausage in a sheet of lasagne and place the rolls close together in a greased foil container. Pour over the sauce and cook in a moderate oven (180°C, 350°F, Gas Mark 4) for 35 minutes.
5 Sprinkle with the cheese before freezing.
6 Reheat from frozen in a moderately hot oven (200°C, 400°F, Gas Mark 6) for about 1 hour.

## Veal and vegetable lasagne

### Makes 4 portions

METRIC/IMPERIAL

| | |
|---|---|
| 225 g/8 oz lasagne | 900-ml/1$\frac{1}{2}$-pint packet golden vegetable soup |
| 2 tablespoons oil | |
| 350 g/12 oz pie veal, cubed | 300 ml/$\frac{1}{2}$ pint water |
| I medium onion, chopped | 300 ml/$\frac{1}{2}$ pint milk |
| I clove garlic, crushed | 175 g/6 oz Cheddar cheese, grated |

1 Cook the lasagne in boiling salted water until tender. Rinse in cold water to separate the strands.
2 Heat the oil and use to sauté the veal, onion and garlic for 10 minutes.
3 Blend the soup mix with the water and milk, and bring to the boil, stirring constantly.
4 Layer the lasagne, meat mixture, vegetable sauce and cheese in a foil container, ending with a layer of cheese.
5 Cool before freezing.
6 Uncover and reheat from frozen in a hot oven (220°C, 425°F, Gas Mark 7) for about 45 minutes.

## Spiced pasta pot

**Makes 4 portions**

METRIC/IMPERIAL
2 tablespoons oil
1 large onion, chopped
2 tablespoons curry powder
1 tablespoon tomato purée

3 tablespoons peanut butter
300 ml/½ pint beef stock
rind of ½ lemon, grated
salt and freshly ground black pepper

*when serving:*
225 g/8 oz spaghetti

1 Heat the oil and use to fry the onion until soft and golden brown. Stir in the curry powder and cook for 5 minutes. Dissolve the tomato purée and peanut butter in the beef stock and add to the pan with the grated lemon rind and seasoning to taste. Cover and cook gently for about 15 minutes, stirring now and then.
2 Freeze in a boiling bag.
3 Cook the spaghetti in a large saucepan of boiling salted water and add the frozen bag of sauce to the same pan. Drain the spaghetti well and stir in the reheated sauce. Serve with grilled pork chipolata sausages or fried fish cakes.

# Rice

## Ham and pepper risotto

**Makes 4 portions**

METRIC/IMPERIAL
3 tablespoons oil
1 medium onion, chopped
2 red peppers, deseeded
225 g/8 oz long grain rice
100 g/4 oz button mushrooms, sliced

750 ml/1¼ pints chicken stock
225 g/8 oz ham, diced
25 g/1 oz sultanas
salt and pepper

1 Heat the oil and use to fry the onion gently until soft but not browned. Chop the red peppers and add to the pan. Fry gently until soft. Stir in the rice and mushrooms and fry for 3 minutes. Pour in the stock and bring to the boil, stirring constantly. Cover and simmer for about 15 minutes, until the rice is just tender and has almost absorbed the liquid.
2 Stir in the ham and sultanas and return to the heat until the liquid is absorbed. Season to taste.
3 Freeze in a boiling bag.
4 Reheat the frozen bag in boiling water for about 25 minutes.

## Prawn and pea risotto

**Makes 4 portions**

METRIC/IMPERIAL
225 g/8 oz long grain rice
2 chicken stock cubes
600 ml/1 pint water
175 g/6 oz peeled prawns

175 g/6 oz frozen peas
100-g/4-oz can crushed pineapple, drained

1 Place the rice, chicken stock cubes and water in a saucepan and bring to the boil.
2 Stir in the prawns and peas, bring back to the boil, cover and simmer for 20 minutes, or until all the liquid is absorbed. Stir in the pineapple.
3 Freeze in a boiling bag.
4 Reheat the frozen bag in boiling water for about 25 minutes.

## Florida chicken risotto

**Makes 4 portions**

METRIC/IMPERIAL
2 tablespoons oil
1 small onion, chopped
225 g/8 oz long grain rice
grated rind and juice of 1 orange
900-ml/1½-pint packet spring vegetable soup

225 g/8 oz cooked chicken, diced
50 g/2 oz mushrooms, sliced

1 Heat the oil, add the onion and rice and sauté for 2 minutes.
2 Make the orange rind and juice up to 900 ml/1½ pints with water and add to the pan with the soup mix.

3 Bring to the boil, stirring constantly. Add the chicken and mushrooms, bring back to the boil, cover and simmer for about 20 minutes, until the liquid is absorbed.
4 Freeze in a boiling bag.
5 Reheat frozen bag in boiling water for about 30 minutes.

## American style paella

### Makes 4 portions
METRIC/IMPERIAL

2 tablespoons oil
I large onion, sliced
225 g/8 oz long grain rice
600 ml/I pint chicken stock
225 g/8 oz frozen mixed vegetables
I teaspoon dry mustard
pinch of powdered saffron
few drops yellow food colouring
salt and pepper
225 g/8 oz cooked chicken, cubed
4 frankfurters, sliced

1 Heat the oil in a saucepan and use to fry the onion until soft. Add the rice and fry for 3 minutes. Add the stock, mixed vegetables, mustard, saffron and food colouring. Season to taste. Bring to the boil and stir once.
2 Cover and simmer for 12 minutes, add the chicken and frankfurters and continue cooking for 3 minutes, or until the rice is tender and the liquid has been absorbed.
3 Freeze in a boiling bag.
4 Reheat frozen bag in boiling water for about 30 minutes.

### Variation:
German-style paella: Substitute 225 g/8 oz diced German boiling sausage and 100 g/4 oz diced pork fillet for the frankfurters and chicken and add them with the stock. Fork through 50 g/2 oz peeled prawns when the risotto is almost cooked.

# Pancakes
## Basic pancakes

### Makes about 24 pancakes
METRIC/IMPERIAL

6 eggs
900 ml/I½ pints milk
350 g/12 oz plain flour
I teaspoon salt
2 tablespoons oil
butter and oil for frying

1 Whisk together the eggs and milk and gradually add the flour, salt and oil, whisking all the time until the mixture is the consistency of smooth thin cream. Allow to stand for up to 1 hour.
2 Heat a little oil and butter in an omelette pan, beat up the batter and use 2 tablespoons to make a thin pancake. Fry until golden brown on both sides. Slide on to a plate.
3 Regrease the pan and continue to make pancakes in the same manner.
4 Use the pancakes in made-up dishes, or freeze in stacks with concertina foil dividers.
5 Allow to defrost in the pack, or spread the pancakes on baking sheets and reheat from frozen in a moderate oven (180°C, 350°F, Gas Mark 4) for about 15 minutes. Alternatively, reheat the pancakes singly in a hot omelette pan without extra fat. Turn once until just heated through.

## Chicken and almond pancakes

### Makes 4 portions
METRIC/IMPERIAL

25 g/I oz butter
2 tablespoons oil
25 g/I oz flaked almonds
100 g/4 oz button mushrooms, sliced
2 tablespoons dry sherry
225 g/8 oz cooked chicken, diced
450 ml/¾ pint savoury white sauce (see page 60)
salt and pepper
8 pancakes
25 g/I oz Cheddar cheese, grated

1 Heat the butter and oil and use to fry the almonds quickly until golden. Drain. Add the mushrooms to the fat in the pan and fry until golden brown.
2 Stir the mushrooms, almonds, sherry and chicken into the white sauce and add seasoning to taste.
3 Divide the filling among the pancakes and roll them up. Place side by side in a foil container and sprinkle with the cheese.
4 Freeze before cooking.
5 Uncover and reheat from frozen in a moderately hot oven (200°C, 400°F, Gas Mark 6) for about 30 minutes.

### Variations:
Smoked haddock pancakes: Substitute 350 g/12 oz cooked and flaked smoked cod or haddock for the chicken, almonds and sherry. Fry the mushrooms in the butter and omit the oil. Season only sparingly with salt.

**Cheese and spinach pancakes:** Substitute 225 g/8 oz cooked and chopped spinach for the chicken and almonds. Use cheese sauce instead of the savoury white sauce.

**Blue cheese and ham pancakes:** Substitute 175 g/6 oz diced ham and 50 g/2 oz crumbled blue cheese for the chicken, almonds and sherry.

## Cheesy fish pancakes

### Makes 4 portions

METRIC/IMPERIAL

| | |
|---|---|
| 25 g/1 oz butter | ½ teaspoon anchovy |
| 2 tablespoons oil | essence |
| 175 g/6 oz button | salt and pepper |
| mushrooms, sliced | 350 g/12 oz cooked coley, |
| 600 ml/1 pint Cheese | flaked |
| sauce (see page 60) | 8 pancakes |

1 Heat the butter and oil and use to fry the mushrooms until golden.
2 Stir the mushroom mixture into half the cheese sauce with the anchovy essence. Season to taste. Fold in the flaked fish.
3 Divide the filling among the pancakes and roll them up. Place side by side in a foil container and pour over the remaining cheese sauce.
4 Freeze before cooking.
5 Uncover and reheat from frozen in a moderately hot oven (200°C, 400°F, Gas Mark 6) for about 30 minutes.

### Variation:

**Sweetcorn and fish pancakes:** Substitute 175 g/6 oz cooked corn kernels for the mushrooms, butter and oil.

# Sandwiches
## Cheese toasting slices

### Makes 8 slices, 8 portions

METRIC/IMPERIAL

| | |
|---|---|
| 225 g/8 oz Lancashire | 100 g/4 oz salami |
| cheese, grated | 1 medium onion, grated |
| 1 tablespoon mayonnaise | 8 slices white bread |
| few drops of Tabasco | |

1 Mix together the cheese, mayonnaise and Tabasco.
2 Chop the salami very finely and add to the mixture with the onion.
3 Slice the bread thickly and cut into 4-cm/1½-inch squares.
4 Toast the slices of bread on one side and spread the cheese mixture on the untoasted sides.
5 Open freeze before packing with dividers.
6 Unwrap and allow to defrost for 1 hour if possible. Grill under moderate heat for about 45 minutes, until well heated through and golden brown on top.

## Sardine and pasta toasts

### Makes 4 toasts, 4 portions

METRIC/IMPERIAL

| | |
|---|---|
| 4 slices white bread | 8 canned sardines |
| 425-g/15-oz can macaroni | 50 g/2 oz Cheddar cheese, |
| cheese | grated |

1 Toast the bread slices on one side and spread the untoasted sides with the macaroni cheese. Top each slice with 2 sardines and sprinkle with cheese. Drizzle over a little sardine oil if wished.
2 Open freeze before packing with dividers.
3 Arrange the toasts on a greased baking sheet and reheat in a moderately hot oven (190°C, 375°F, Gas Mark 5) for about 15 minutes, until well heated through and the cheese has melted.

## Ham, cheese and egg snacks

### Makes 4 snacks, 4 portions

METRIC/IMPERIAL

| | |
|---|---|
| 4 slices white bread | 4 large slices Gouda |
| 2 teaspoons mild mustard | cheese |
| 4 slices ham | |

*when serving:*

| | |
|---|---|
| 50 g/2 oz butter | oil for frying |
| 4 eggs | |

1 Trim the bread slices and spread lightly with mustard. Top each piece of bread with a slice of ham and then a slice of cheese.
2 Pack with dividers for freezing.
3 Melt one quarter of the butter and use to gently fry a snack for about 5 minutes, until the cheese begins to melt. Drain well and keep warm while you fry the remaining snacks. If the pan is big enough, fry more than one at a time.

**4** Meanwhile, fry the eggs in oil in a separate pan. Top each snack with a fried egg before serving.

**Variations:**

**Sausage, cheese and egg snacks:** Spread the bread slices with sweet brown pickles instead of mustard and use 4 large pork sausages in place of the ham. Fry the sausages then slice and arrange on the bread.

**Tomato, cheese and bacon snacks:** Spread the bread slices with piccalilli and use 4 large sliced tomatoes instead of the ham. Top each snack with 2 rashers of crisply fried streaky bacon before serving.

## Cream cheese and apple loaf

**Makes 3–4 portions**

METRIC/IMPERIAL

| | |
|---|---|
| I medium French loaf | I clove garlic |
| 225 g/8 oz cream cheese | salt and black pepper |
| 50 g/2 oz butter, softened | 175 g/6 oz smoked |
| I tablespoon chopped parsley |    Continental sausage **or** cooked ham |
| I tablespoon chopped chives | 3 tablespoons sweet brown pickle |
| 3 dessert apples, peeled | |

**1** Cut the loaf in half lengthwise and remove a little of the soft bread inside.

**2** Beat together the cream cheese and butter then work in the herbs.

**3** Core and chop the apples. Very finely chop the garlic and add to the cheese mixture with the apple and seasoning to taste.

**4** Divide this mixture between the two pieces of bread and spread evenly. Cover one piece with slices of sausage or ham and the other with the pickle and sandwich both pieces together to reshape the loaf.

**5** Cut into portions or leave whole before freezing.

**6** Defrost but keep cool.

## Cheese and chutney dreams

**Makes 4 portions**

METRIC/IMPERIAL

| | |
|---|---|
| 8 slices white bread | chutney, chopped |
| butter for spreading | 4 slices processed cheese |
| 4 tablespoons mango | |

*when serving:*
oil for frying

**1** Trim the slices of bread and spread with butter and mango chutney. Place a slice of cheese on each of 4 pieces of bread and sandwich together with the remaining pieces. Cut each sandwich into 4 triangles.

**2** Pack with dividers for freezing.

**3** Shallow fry from frozen in hot oil for about 5 minutes, until golden brown on both sides.

Fortunately there is no need to elaborate on the many fillings suitable for frozen sandwiches since the only unsuitable items make such a short list. These include sliced or chopped hard-boiled egg and any salad vegetables such as lettuce, tomatoes and cucumber. A small amount of salad cream or mayonnaise is satisfactory when used just to bind other ingredients together to make a good spreading consistency. Sandwiches can be trimmed or packed with the crusts on and carefully labelled. This is especially useful if you wish to make mixed packs for various members of the family to take away from home and cater to their individual tastes.

## Savoury sandwich selection

For a change, make up a savoury butter using 1–2 teaspoons of yeast extract spread to each 25 g/1 oz of butter or margarine. Just beat together and use to spread the bread slices. Allow approximately 100g/4 oz butter or margarine for spreading each large sliced loaf.

**Suggested fillings:**

1 Slices of corned beef with well-drained pickled red cabbage.

2 Slices of tongue and horseradish sauce.

3 Slices of cheese with thinly sliced stuffed green olives.

4 Mashed tuna mixed with a squeeze of lemon juice and a little salad cream.

## Double decker sandwiches

These are made with 3 slices of bread per sandwich; either 2 white and 1 brown or 2 brown and 1 white, with the odd man out going in the centre. Spread the slices of bread with butter. Sandwich 2 slices together with any freezable pickle or relish. Spread the top of the sandwich with more butter then cover with either slices of cheese, any cold roast meat, mashed sardines, pilchards, or flaked canned salmon. Top with the third slice of bread. Press well together

# Made-up dishes

## Tuna curry

### Makes 4 portions

METRIC/IMPERIAL

50 g/2 oz butter
1 medium onion, chopped
1 tablespoon curry
  powder
225-g/8-oz can tomatoes,
  chopped
250 ml/8 fl oz water

1 tablespoon seedless
  raisins
200-g/7-oz can tuna
rind of 1 lemon, finely
  grated
2 tablespoons lemon juice
1 tablespoon cornflour
salt

*when serving:*
225 g/8 oz long grain rice

1 Melt the butter and use to fry the onion gently until soft. Stir in the curry powder and cook for 2 minutes. Add the tomatoes and their liquid, the water, raisins, flaked tuna and oil from the can. Bring to the boil, add the lemon rind and juice, cover and simmer for 10 minutes, stirring occasionally.
2 Moisten the cornflour with a little cold water, add to the pan and bring back to the boil, stirring constantly. Cook for 2 minutes and season with salt to taste.
3 Freeze in a boiling bag.
4 Bring a pan of salted water to the boil, add the frozen bag of curry, bring back to the boil and cook gently for 10 minutes. Add the rice to the water with the bag of curry in it and cook gently until the rice is tender. The curry will then be reheated.

## Tuna and asparagus savoury

### Makes 4 portions

METRIC/IMPERIAL

100 g/4 oz small pasta
  shapes
2 tablespoons oil,
1 medium onion, chopped
900-ml/1½-pint packet
  asparagus soup

450 ml/¾ pint water
150 ml/¼ pint milk
200-g/7-oz can tuna,
  drained
salt and pepper

1 Cook the pasta in boiling salted water until tender. Drain well.
2 Heat the oil and use to fry the onion gently until soft but not brown. Stir in the soup mix, water and milk and bring to the boil, stirring constantly. Cook for 5 minutes.
3 Flake the tuna and fold into the sauce with the cooked pasta. Season to taste.
4 Freeze in a boiling bag.
5 Reheat the frozen bag in boiling water for about 30 minutes.

## Oaty pilchard cakes

### Makes 4 portions

METRIC/IMPERIAL

425-g/15-oz can pilchards
  in tomato sauce
1 teaspoon
  Worcestershire sauce
225 g/8 oz mashed
  potato

2 tablespoons flour
salt and pepper
1 egg, beaten
1 tablespoon water
75 g/3 oz rolled oats

*when serving:*
oil for frying

1 Drain the pilchards and remove the bones. Mash with the Worcestershire sauce, potato and flour until well blended. Add a little of the tomato sauce from the can if the mixture is too stiff. Season to taste with salt and pepper.
2 Divide the mixture into 8 equal portions and shape each into a round flat cake.
3 Beat together the egg and water, use to coat the cakes, then cover with the oats.
4 Open freeze, then pack in layers with dividers.
5 Deep fry from frozen in hot oil for about 5 minutes, until golden brown and crisp.

### Variation:

**Cheesy pilchard cakes:** Add 50 g/2 oz grated strong Cheddar cheese to the fish mixture and use soft breadcrumbs instead of the oats.

## Quickie fish with peanuts

### Makes 4 portions

METRIC/IMPERIAL

little oil for frying
4 frozen breaded cod
  portions

100 g/4 oz salted peanuts
50 g/2 oz butter
wedges of lemon

1 Heat the oil and use to fry the fish portions for about 10 minutes, until golden brown on both sides. Remove to a warm serving dish.
2 Finely chop the peanuts. Melt the butter, stir in the nuts and heat gently for about 3 minutes.
3 Spoon the peanut and butter mixture over the fish portions and garnish with lemon wedges.

## Corned beef patties

### Makes 4 portions

METRIC/IMPERIAL

350-g/12-oz can corned
  beef
1 large onion, grated
1 tablespoon spicy brown
  table sauce

50 g/2 oz rolled oats
salt and pepper
little beaten egg

*when serving:*
oil for frying

1 Mash the corned beef and mix with the onion, brown sauce and rolled oats. Season with salt and pepper and bind the mixture with a little beaten egg.
2 With floured hands, divide the mixture into 8 equal portions and shape into round flat cakes.
3 Freeze with dividers.
4 Shallow fry the patties from frozen in hot oil for about 5 minutes on each side, until golden brown.

## Herbed gnocchi in tomato

### Makes 4 portions

METRIC/IMPERIAL

| | |
|---|---|
| 600 ml/1 pint milk | 150 ml/¼ pint chicken |
| 100 g/4 oz fine semolina | stock |
| I teaspoon dried basil | 2 tablespoons tomato |
| ¾ teaspoon salt | purée |
| 50 g/2 oz butter | I tablespoon brown sugar |
| I egg, beaten | I teaspoon cornflour |
| 175 g/6 oz strong | salt and pepper |
| Cheddar cheese, grated | |

1 Bring the milk to the boil and sprinkle on the semolina, herbs and salt. Stir and cook over moderate heat until the mixture is thick and smooth.
2 Remove from the heat and beat in the butter, egg, and three-quarters of the cheese. Mix well.
3 Spread the mixture about 0·5 cm/¼ inch thick on non-stick vegetable parchment or greased foil and cool. Cut into squares or fancy shapes and arrange in a greased foil container.
4 Meanwhile, place the stock, tomato purée and sugar in a saucepan and bring to the boil. Moisten the cornflour with a little cold water, add to the pan and bring back to the boil, stirring constantly. Season to taste, pour over the gnocchi and sprinkle with the remaining cheese.
5 Open freeze before covering.
6 Uncover and reheat from frozen in a moderately hot oven (200°C, 400°F, Gas Mark 6) for about 40 minutes.

## Crispy chicken croquettes

### Makes 4 portions

METRIC/IMPERIAL

| | |
|---|---|
| 50 g/2 oz butter | ¼ teaspoon ground nutmeg |
| 100 g/4 oz mushrooms, | salt and pepper |
| chopped | 300 ml/½ pint basic |
| 40 g/1½ oz flour | pancake batter (see |
| 250 ml/8 fl oz milk | page 47) |
| I egg yolk | oil for frying |
| 450 g/1 lb cooked | |
| chicken, minced | |

1 Melt the butter and use to fry the mushrooms for 3 minutes. Stir in the flour and cook for 2 minutes. Gradually add the milk and bring to the boil, stirring constantly, until the mixture is smooth and thick. Remove from the heat and beat in the egg yolk, chicken, nutmeg and seasoning to taste. Cool.
2 Divide the mixture into 12 portions and shape each into a croquette shape. Dip in the pancake batter and deep fry in hot oil for about 4 minutes, until pale golden brown. Drain well.
3 Freeze in layers with dividers.
4 Arrange the croquettes spread out on a greased baking sheet and reheat from frozen in a hot oven (220°C, 425°F, Gas Mark 7) for about 20 minutes, until crisp and golden brown.

**Variation:**
**Turkey and onion croquettes:** Substitute cooked turkey for the chicken and use 1 large onion, chopped, instead of the mushrooms. Season with salt and black pepper.

## Ham and celery supper dish

### Makes 4 portions

METRIC/IMPERIAL

| | |
|---|---|
| 4 small celery hearts | 2 tablespoons chopped |
| 300 ml/½ pint water | parsley |
| I chicken stock cube | salt and pepper |
| 3 tablespoons evaporated | 4 slices ham |
| milk | 75 g/3 oz Cheddar cheese, |
| 25 g/1 oz butter | grated |
| 25 g/1 oz flour | |

1 Place the celery hearts in a saucepan with the water and stock cube. Bring to the boil, cover and simmer for about 45 minutes, until the celery is tender.
2 Remove the celery from the pan and drain well. Make the cooking liquid up to 300 ml/½ pint with the evaporated milk and more water if necessary.
3 Melt the butter and stir in the flour. Gradually add the measured liquid and bring to the boil, stirring constantly. Stir in the parsley and adjust the seasoning if necessary.
4 Wrap each celery heart in a slice of ham and arrange in a greased foil container. Pour over the sauce and sprinkle with the cheese.
5 Open freeze before covering.
6 Uncover and reheat from frozen in a moderately hot oven (200°C, 400°F, Gas Mark 6) for about 40 minutes.

**Variation:**
**Complete celery and ham supper:** Cook 100 g/4 oz small pasta shapes in salted water until tender. Drain well, stir in 1 teaspoon oil and arrange in the container with the ham and celery before covering with the sauce. Omit the parsley.

## Peanut butter chicken portions

### Makes 8 portions

METRIC/IMPERIAL

| | |
|---|---|
| 100 g/4 oz peanut butter | 8 chicken portions |
| 2 eggs, beaten | 50 g/2 oz flour |
| 2 teaspoons salt | 100 g/4 oz dry |
| ¼ teaspoon pepper | breadcrumbs |
| 150 ml/¼ pint milk | 4 tablespoons oil |

1 Beat together the peanut butter, eggs, salt and pepper. Gradually beat in the milk.
2 Coat the chicken portions with flour, dip into the peanut butter mixture and then cover with breadcrumbs.
3 Use some of the oil to grease a large roasting tin and arrange the coated chicken portions on it. Drizzle over the remaining oil.
4 Bake in a moderately hot oven (190°C, 375°F, Gas Mark 5) for about 40 minutes, or until tender.
5 Mould each portion carefully in foil, then pack together in a polythene container for freezing.
6 Defrost and then arrange the foil-wrapped portions on a baking sheet. Reheat in a hot oven (220°C, 425°F, Gas Mark 7) for 10 minutes, then carefully open up the foil parcels and return to the oven for a further 10–15 minutes, until golden brown and well heated through.

## Tomatoes stuffed with crab

**Makes 4 portions**

METRIC/IMPERIAL
| | |
|---|---|
| 4 large tomatoes | pinch of curry powder |
| 75-g/3-oz can dressed crab | 1 tablespoon mayonnaise |
| 25 g/1 oz soft breadcrumbs | salt and pepper |

1 Cut a thin slice from the top of each tomato and scoop out the seeds, keeping the shell intact.
2 Mix together the crab, breadcrumbs, curry powder and mayonnaise with seasoning to taste.
3 Fill the tomato shells with the crab stuffing and put back the lids.
4 Arrange the tomatoes in a foil container and bake in a moderate oven (180°C, 350°F, Gas Mark 4) for 10 minutes.
5 Open freeze then cover with foil.
6 Reheat from frozen, still covered, in a moderate oven as above for about 15 minutes, or until well heated through.

### Variations:

**Chicken and pasta stuffed tomatoes:** Substitute a filling of 75 g/3 oz cooked small pasta shapes mixed with 50 g/2 oz chopped cooked chicken, 1 tablespoon chopped canned red pimento, and seasoned with garlic salt and pepper to taste.

**Tuna and rice stuffed tomatoes:** Substitute a filling of 75 g/3 oz cooked rice mixed with 50 g/2 oz flaked tuna, 4 chopped black olives, $\frac{1}{2}$ teaspoon lemon juice and seasoned with salt and black pepper.

**Beefy stuffed tomatoes:** Substitute a filling of 75 g/3 oz cooked minced beef mixed with 1 tablespoon tomato ketchup and seasoned with salt and pepper to taste.

## Salmon and corn cakes

**Makes 8 cakes, 4 portions**

METRIC/IMPERIAL
| | |
|---|---|
| 450 g/1 lb mashed potato | 196-g/7-oz can sweetcorn kernels, drained |
| 25 g/1 oz butter | 1 large egg, beaten |
| salt and pepper | toasted breadcrumbs for coating |
| 196-g/7-oz can pink salmon, drained | |

*when serving:*
oil for frying

1 Beat the potato until smooth with the butter and seasoning. Bone and flake the salmon and add to the potato with the sweetcorn. Chill until the mixture is firm.
2 Divide the salmon mixture into 8 portions and shape each into a round flat cake.
3 Dip the cakes in the beaten egg and coat all over with the breadcrumbs.
4 Pack with dividers for freezing.
5 Shallow fry from frozen in hot oil for about 8 minutes, until golden brown on both sides.

## Nutty corned beef pot

**Makes 4 portions**

METRIC/IMPERIAL
| | |
|---|---|
| 1 medium onion, sliced | 3 tablespoons tomato ketchup |
| 50 g/2 oz celery heart, sliced | 50 g/2 oz salted peanuts, chopped |
| 300 ml/½ pint beef stock | 196-g/7-oz can corned beef, diced |
| 100 g/4 oz canned or frozen sweetcorn kernels | pepper |

1 Place the onion and celery in a saucepan with the stock and cook gently for about 20 minutes, until the vegetables are tender. Stir in the sweetcorn and cook for a further 5 minutes. Add the tomato ketchup, peanuts and corned beef and heat gently for 5 minutes. Season with pepper to taste.
2 Freeze in a boiling bag.
3 Reheat frozen bag in boiling water for about 30 minutes.

# Sausages

## Ratatouille sausages

**Makes 4–6 portions**

METRIC/IMPERIAL
I green pepper, deseeded
I red pepper, deseeded
100 g/4 oz butter
I large onion, sliced
450 g/I lb tomatoes, chopped
I medium aubergine, diced
175 g/6 oz button

mushrooms, sliced
225 g/8 oz courgettes, sliced
150 ml/¼ pint beef stock
450 g/I lb chipolata sausages
2 tablespoons oil
salt and pepper

1 Slice the peppers and cook in the butter with the onion until beginning to soften. Add the tomatoes, aubergine, mushrooms, courgettes and stock and cook gently for about 30 minutes, or until the vegetables are tender.
2 Meanwhile, fry the sausages in the oil until golden brown all over and cooked through. Slice them thickly and add to the ratatouille. Season to taste.
3 Pack in a polythene container for freezing.
4 Turn the mixture into a saucepan, add 2 tablespoons water and reheat very gently, stirring frequently, until piping hot. Adjust the seasoning if necessary.

**Variations:**

Ratatouille lamb: Substitute 450 g/I lb diced boneless lamb for the sausages and fry with the onion and pepper before adding the rest of the vegetables.

Ratatouille chicken: Substitute 450 g/I lb cooked diced chicken for the sausages. Fold it into the cooked ratatouille before freezing. Freeze in a boiling bag and reheat the frozen bag in boiling water for about 30 minutes (otherwise the chicken will break down when being reheated in the saucepan).

Ratatouille with luncheon meat: Substitute a diced 350-g/12-oz can of luncheon meat for the sausages. Fold it into the cooked ratatouille before freezing.

Ratatouille with frankfurters: Substitute 350 g/12 oz sliced frankfurter sausages for the chipolata sausages and fold into the ratatouille before freezing.

## Hungarian sausages

**Makes 4 portions**

METRIC/IMPERIAL
2 tablespoons oil
I large onion, chopped
I tablespoon sweet paprika pepper
I tablespoon seasoned flour
450 ml/¾ pint beef stock

I tablespoon tomato purée
450 g/I lb beef sausages
225 g/8 oz potato, diced
225 g/8 oz carrot, sliced
salt

1 Heat the oil and use to fry the onion gently until soft. Stir in the paprika pepper and cook for 2 minutes. Sprinkle in the flour and stir well. Gradually add the stock and tomato purée and bring to the boil, stirring constantly.
2 Add the sausages, potato, and carrot to the pan and bring back to the boil. Cover and simmer for about 30 minutes. Season to taste with salt.
3 Freeze in a polythene container.
4 Turn frozen into a saucepan, add 2 tablespoons water and reheat very gently, stirring frequently, until piping hot.

## Sausage and mushroom bake

**Makes 4 portions**

METRIC/IMPERIAL
2 rashers streaky bacon, derinded
I small onion, chopped
50 g/2 oz butter
350 g/12 oz pork sausagemeat
2 tablespoons chopped parsley

50 g/2 oz fresh crumbs
I egg, beaten
12 large flat mushrooms
salt and pepper
150 ml/¼ pint single cream
50 g/2 oz Cheddar cheese, grated

1 Chop the bacon and fry with the onion in the butter until the onion is soft. Combine this mixture with the sausagemeat, parsley, breadcrumbs and beaten egg.
2 Remove the mushroom stalks, chop them and add to the sausagemeat mixture with seasoning to taste.
3 Place the mushroom caps in a greased foil container and cover with the sausagemeat mixture. Pour over the cream and sprinkle with the cheese.
4 Freeze before cooking.
5 Cook from frozen in a moderately hot oven (190°C, 375°F, Gas Mark 5) for about 1 hour.

## Sausages with creamy mushrooms

**Makes 4 portions**

METRIC/IMPERIAL
50 g/2 oz butter
450 g/I lb beef chipolata sausages
I large onion, sliced
100 g/4 oz mushrooms, sliced

2 tablespoons flour
300 ml/½ pint beef stock
salt and pepper

when serving:
150 ml/¼ pint soured cream

1 Melt the butter and use to fry the sausages gently for about 10 minutes, until golden brown all over. Remove from the pan and keep warm.
2 Add the onion to the fat remaining in the pan and fry gently until soft. Add the mushrooms and cook for

a further 5 minutes. Sprinkle in the flour and stir well. Gradually add the stock and bring to the boil, stirring constantly. Season to taste and stir in the sausages.

3 Freeze in a polythene container.

4 Turn into a saucepan and reheat very gently from frozen, stirring frequently, until the mixture comes to the boil. Stir in the cream and reheat. Adjust the seasoning if necessary.

## Sausage burgers with apple and leek

### Makes 4 portions

METRIC/IMPERIAL

| | |
|---|---|
| 450 g/1 lb pork sausagemeat | 2 tablespoons well seasoned flour |
| ¼ teaspoon curry powder | 1 tablespoon oil |
| 1 tablespoon tomato ketchup | 2 large cooking apples, peeled |
| 1 tablespoon spicy brown table sauce | 25 g/1 oz butter |
| salt and pepper | 2 large leeks, sliced |
| | 300 ml/½ pint apple juice |

1 Mix together the sausagemeat, curry powder, ketchup, brown sauce and seasoning to taste. Divide into 8 portions, shape each into a round flat burger and coat in seasoned flour.

2 Heat the oil and use to fry the cakes until golden brown on both sides.

3 Meanwhile, core and slice the apples. Melt the butter, add the apple and leek and cook for 5 minutes.

4 Transfer to a foil container and top with the burgers. Pour in the apple juice and cook in a moderate oven (160°C, 325°F, Gas Mark 3) for 35 minutes.

5 Cover with foil before freezing.

6 Place still covered in a moderately hot oven (200°C, 400°F, Gas Mark 6) for 30 minutes, remove the foil and return to the oven for a further 20 minutes, until well heated through.

# Meatless dishes

## Nutty courgettes

### Makes 4–6 portions

METRIC/IMPERIAL

| | |
|---|---|
| 50 g/2 oz butter | 1 tablespoon soft brown sugar |
| 1 large onion, grated | salt and pepper |
| 1·5 kg/3 lb courgettes, sliced | 150 ml/¼ pint boiling water |
| 2 cloves of garlic, crushed | 50g/2 oz salted peanuts |
| 3 tablespoons tomato purée | |

1 Melt the butter and use to fry the onion and courgettes gently until soft. Add the garlic, tomato purée, sugar and seasoning to taste. Gradually add the boiling water, stirring constantly.

2 Bring to the boil, cover and simmer for 10 minutes or until the courgettes are just tender.

3 Add the nuts and cook for a further 2 minutes.

4 Freeze in polythene containers.

5 Defrost and then reheat in a saucepan. If reheating from frozen, stir frequently to avoid burning.

## Surprise vegetable scramble

### Makes 4 portions

METRIC/IMPERIAL

| | |
|---|---|
| 1 green pepper, deseeded | 1 clove of garlic, crushed |
| 1 large onion, chopped | 1 teaspoon dried mixed herbs |
| 50 g/2 oz margarine | salt and pepper |
| 1 large marrow, peeled | |
| 2 canned red pimentos, chopped | |

*when serving:*

| | |
|---|---|
| 4 eggs, beaten | 4 slices hot buttered toast |
| 150 ml/¼ pint soured cream | |

1 Chop the pepper and fry with the onion in the margarine until soft.

2 Deseed and chop the marrow and add to the pan with the pimento, garlic, herbs and seasoning. Cook gently, stirring frequently, for about 15 minutes, or until the marrow is tender.

3 Freeze in polythene containers.

4 Reheat from frozen in a saucepan stirring now and then. When the mixture is at boiling point, fold in the egg and soured cream and heat gently stirring until the eggs begin to scramble.

5 Serve the mixture piled on the slices of buttered toast.

# Soups, sauces and starters

Soups and sauces with a high water content present little problem on defrosting because they can easily be turned out of their containers. However, they do require an adequate headspace when being packed for the freezer to allow for expansion of the water content as it freezes. Whether you pack in a rigid-based container with a seal or in a bag, allow about one tenth of the total volume as a headspace. Otherwise the seal might be forced off or the twist tie on the bag forced open. Treat soups and sauces carefully, liquids which spill in the freezer are the most frequent cause of having to defrost before it is strictly necessary. To save space, reduce soups rather than making and freezing them at serving strength. It is more sensible to add a little extra liquid, even water, to dilute them on reheating.

### Packing terrines and pâtés

Sometimes it is useful to pack pâtés in individual dishes so that they may be served straight from the freezer. Terrines, being larger, take some time to defrost and might provide too great a quantity to serve at one meal. If the cooked terrine or pâté can be turned out, it is comparatively easy to divide into wedges or thick slices and re-pack with dividers so that individual portions can be taken out as required. Or portions can merely be scooped out on to a square of foil and wrapped into a neat parcel to be included in packed lunches or used as a sandwich filling. A small amount of pâté can quickly be converted into an exotic dinner party starter if enclosed in fleurons which are very simple to make. Cut out 5-cm/2-inch circles of thinly-rolled puff pastry, brush with beaten egg and fold over to make half-moons. Place on a greased baking sheet, glaze again with egg and bake in a hot oven (220°C, 425°F, Gas Mark 7) for 15 minutes, until golden brown. Cool and split. Any soft pâté or one that is softened by beating in a little single cream can be piped into this split ready for serving. Fish mousses and cheese mousses are just as delicious for this purpose as ones made with chicken livers or meat. Of course frozen puff pastry is convenient and gives consistently good results.

### Menu planning for meals

Any meal which extends to three courses requires some sort of work plan to ensure that all the food is ready at the right time. Make it easy for yourself by serving starters straight from the freezer, or soups which only require reheating with a little added liquid rather than cooking. Cold soups are also great trouble savers. They should be transferred to the refrigerator in time to thaw out and allow for whisking if necessary to restore the texture, then served slightly chilled.

# Soups

## Florida tomato soup

**Makes 4–6 portions**

METRIC/IMPERIAL
50 g/2 oz butter
I large onion, grated
40 g/1½ oz flour
600 ml/I pint chicken
  stock
425-g/15-oz can tomatoes,
  sieved

*when serving:*
150 ml/¼ pint soured
  cream

¼ teaspoon dried
  marjoram
½ teaspoon
  Worcestershire sauce
finely grated rind and
  juice of I large orange
salt and pepper

1 Melt the butter and use to fry the onion gently until soft but not coloured. Stir in the flour and cook for 2 minutes. Gradually add the stock and sieved tomatoes and their liquid. Bring to the boil, stirring constantly.
2 Add the marjoram, Worcestershire sauce and orange rind and juice. Cover and simmer for about 15 minutes, then season to taste.
3 Freeze in polythene containers.
4 Reheat from frozen in a saucepan, stirring frequently. When the soup is at boiling point, check the seasoning and stir in the soured cream.

## Spinach and leek soup

**Makes 4–6 portions**

METRIC/IMPERIAL
450 g/I lb spinach
600 ml/I pint chicken
  stock
50 g/2 oz butter
I medium onion, chopped

I large leek, sliced
40 g/1½ oz flour
¼ teaspoon ground mace
450 ml/¾ pint milk
salt and pepper

1 Prepare the spinach and place in a saucepan with the stock. Bring to the boil, cover and simmer for about 10 minutes, or until tender. Liquidize or sieve.
2 Meanwhile, in a clean saucepan, melt the butter and use to fry the onion and leek gently until soft but not coloured. Stir in the flour and mace and cook for 2 minutes. Gradually add the spinach mixture and the milk and bring to the boil, stirring constantly. Simmer for 5 minutes and season to taste.
3 Freeze in polythene containers.
4 Reheat from frozen in a saucepan, stirring frequently, Add a little extra milk if the soup is too thick.

## Jerusalem artichoke soup

**Makes 8 portions**

METRIC/IMPERIAL
75 g/3 oz butter
I large onion, chopped
0·75 kg/1½ lb Jerusalem
  artichokes
I litre/1¾ pints chicken
  stock

finely grated rind and juice
  of ½ lemon
I teaspoon sugar
2 tablespoons cornflour
150 ml/¼ pint milk
salt and pepper

1 Melt the butter and use to fry the onion gently until soft. Peel the artichokes, slice and add to the pan. Cover and cook gently for 10 minutes, shaking the pan occasionally. Add the stock, lemon rind and juice and the sugar. Bring to the boil, cover and simmer for 20 minutes. Cool.
2 Liquidise or sieve the soup and return to the rinsed-out saucepan.
3 Blend the cornflour with the milk, add to the pan and bring to the boil, stirring constantly. Cook for 2 minutes and adjust the seasoning. Cool.
4 Freeze in polythene tumblers.
5 Turn the frozen soup into a saucepan and reheat slowly to boiling point, stirring frequently. Adjust the seasoning if necessary.

## Pea soup with ham

**Makes 8 portions**

METRIC/IMPERIAL
450 g/I lb dried peas
generous I litre/2 pints
  ham or chicken stock*
I large onion, sliced
I large carrot, sliced

I small swede, diced
4 sticks celery, sliced
100 g/4 oz ham, diced
salt and pepper

1 Cover the peas with cold water and allow to soak overnight.
2 The next day, drain the peas and place in a large saucepan with the stock, onion, carrot, swede and celery. Bring to the boil, cover and simmer for 2 hours, or until the peas are soft.
3 Liquidise or sieve the soup, stir in the ham and season to taste.
4 Freeze in polythene tumblers.
5 Turn the frozen soup into a saucepan and reheat very gently, stirring frequently, until boiling. Adjust the seasoning if necessary and add a little milk if the soup is too thick.

**\*Note:**

All ham stock may be too salty for this hearty soup. If it is available, use half stock and half water then season carefully after cooking.

# Corn and bacon chowder

## Makes 4–6 portions

METRIC/IMPERIAL

| | |
|---|---|
| 175 g/6 oz streaky bacon, derinded | 25 g/1 oz butter |
| 1 large onion, chopped | 25 g/1 oz flour |
| 3 sticks celery, chopped | 600 ml/1 pint milk |
| 1 canned red pimento, chopped | 325-g/11½-oz can sweetcorn kernels |
| 450 ml/¾ pint water | salt and pepper |

1 Snip up the bacon and fry gently until it is crisp and the fat runs freely. Add the onion and celery and fry gently until the celery is beginning to soften. Add the pimento and water and bring to the boil. Cover and simmer for about 30 minutes, until the vegetables are tender.
2 Melt the butter in a clean saucepan and stir in the flour. Cook for 2 minutes. Gradually add the milk and the liquid from the can of sweetcorn and bring to the boil, stirring constantly. Simmer for 2 minutes and stir in the sweetcorn. Add the contents of the pan with the bacon mixture in it, stir well and season to taste.
3 Freeze in polythene containers.
4 Defrost and then reheat in a saucepan. If reheating from frozen, add a little extra milk and stir all the time to help prevent the soup from sticking and burning.

# Curried apple soup

## Makes 6–8 portions

METRIC/IMPERIAL

| | |
|---|---|
| 450 g/1 lb dessert apples | generous 1 litre/2 pints chicken stock |
| 2 tablespoons lemon juice | |
| 50 g/2 oz butter | ½ teaspoon finely grated lemon rind |
| 1 medium onion, chopped | |
| 25 g/1 oz flour | salt |
| 2 teaspoons curry powder | |

*when serving:*

| | |
|---|---|
| 150 ml/¼ pint natural yogurt | fried bread croûtons |

1 Peel, core and roughly chop the apples and sprinkle with the lemon juice.
2 Melt the butter and use to fry the onion gently until soft. Stir in the flour and curry powder and cook for 2 minutes. Gradually add the stock and bring to the boil, stirring constantly. Add the prepared apple and the lemon rind, bring back to the boil and stir well. Cover and simmer for about 40 minutes, stirring occasionally.
3 Liquidise the soup and add salt to taste.
4 Freeze in polythene containers.
5 Reheat from frozen in a saucepan and when the soup is at boiling point, stir in the yogurt until well blended. Check the seasoning and serve sprinkled with fried bread croutons.

# Lemony leek soup

## Makes 6–8 portions

METRIC/IMPERIAL

| | |
|---|---|
| 50 g/2 oz margarine | 2 large potatoes, sliced |
| 1 large onion, chopped | ½ teaspoon dried oregano |
| 1·5 kg/3 lb leeks, chopped | finely grated rind and juice of 1 lemon |
| 2 chicken stock cubes | |
| generous 1 litre/2 pints water | ½ teaspoon ground nutmeg |
| | salt and pepper |

*when serving:*

| | |
|---|---|
| 150 ml/¼ pint single cream | 1 tablespoon chives, chopped |

1 Melt the margarine and use to fry the onion and leek gently until soft.
2 Add the crumbled stock cubes, water, potato, oregano, lemon rind and juice, nutmeg and seasoning.
3 Bring to the boil, stirring constantly, cover and simmer for about 20 minutes.
4 Liquidise and adjust the seasoning before freezing in polythene containers.
5 Defrost and then stir in the cream. Serve sprinkled with the chives. If required hot, reheat from frozen in a saucepan then add the cream and chives.

# Onion and fish soup

## Makes 4 portions

METRIC/IMPERIAL

| | |
|---|---|
| 225 g/8 oz diced potato | 50 g/2 oz butter |
| 100 g/4 oz coley, skinned | salt and pepper |
| 2 large onions, sliced | |
| 1 litre/1¾ pints chicken stock | |

*when serving:*

| | |
|---|---|
| 150 ml/¼ pint soured cream | |

1 Place the potato, coley and half the onion in a saucepan with the stock. Bring to the boil, cover and simmer for about 30 minutes. Strain.
2 In the rinsed out saucepan melt the butter and use to fry the remaining onion gently until soft but not coloured. Add the strained soup, stir well and season to taste.
3 Freeze in polythene containers.
4 Reheat from frozen in a saucepan, stirring frequently. When the soup comes to boiling point, stir in the cream and remove from the heat. Adjust the seasoning if necessary.

## Beefy minestrone

### Makes 6–8 portions

METRIC/IMPERIAL
50 g/2 oz butter
100 g/4 oz minced beef
2 carrots, chopped
1 large onion, chopped
3 large sticks celery, sliced
1 large potato, diced
100 g/4 oz white cabbage, shredded

2 chicken stock cubes
1·75 litres/3 pints water
2 tablespoons tomato ketchup
1 teaspoon dried basil
75 g/3 oz tiny pasta shapes
salt and pepper

1 Melt the butter in a large saucepan, add the minced beef and fry briskly, stirring constantly, until browned and crumbly. Add the prepared vegetables and cook for 8 minutes, stirring frequently.
2 Add the crumbled stock cubes, water, tomato ketchup and herbs. Bring to the boil, then simmer for 50 minutes.
3 Add the pasta to the soup, stir well and simmer for a further 10 minutes, or until the pasta and vegetables are cooked. Season to taste.
4 Freeze in polythene containers.
5 Defrost and then reheat in a saucepan to boiling point, stirring frequently.


## Game and vegetable soup

### Makes 6–8 portions

METRIC/IMPERIAL
3 tablespoons oil
2 grouse or pheasant carcasses and 1 small wood pigeon, split *or* 2 small wood pigeons, split
100 g/4 oz stewing steak
1 medium onion, chopped
1 large carrot, sliced

4 sticks of celery, sliced
3 beef stock cubes
1·75 litres/3 pints boiling water
2 bouquet garnis
salt and pepper
40 g/1½ oz butter
40 g/1½ oz flour
4 tablespoons dry sherry

1 Heat the oil and use to brown the carcasses and pigeon on all sides. Place in a large saucepan. Add the steak to the fat remaining in the pan and fry until browned on both sides. Add the vegetables and cook for 5 minutes, stirring frequently. Transfer to the saucepan with the stock cubes, water, bouquets garnis and seasoning to taste. Bring to the boil, cover and simmer for about 1½ hours.
2 Strain the mixture carefully, remove any flesh from the carcasses and the pigeon and cut into small pieces. Chop the beef.
3 Melt the butter in a clean saucepan and stir in the flour. Cook for 1 minute. Gradually add the strained soup and bring to the boil, stirring constantly. Add the chopped meat and the sherry and adjust the seasoning.
4 Freeze in polythene containers.
5 Reheat gently from frozen in a saucepan, stirring frequently. Simmer for 5 minutes and check the seasoning.


## Marvellous cauliflower soup

### Makes 6–8 portions

METRIC/IMPERIAL
1 large cauliflower
1 litre/1¾ pints chicken stock
25 g/1 oz butter
25 g/1 oz flour

½ teaspoon ground nutmeg
salt and pepper
150 ml/¼ pint single cream

1 Divide the cauliflower into florets and place in a saucepan with the stock. Bring to the boil, cover and simmer for about 20 minutes, until the cauliflower is soft. Liquidise or sieve.
2 In a clean saucepan, melt the butter and stir in the flour and nutmeg. Cook for 1 minute. Gradually add the cauliflower mixture and bring to the boil, stirring constantly. Cook for 5 minutes, stirring frequently. Season to taste, stir in the cream and remove from the heat.
3 Freeze in polythene containers.
4 Reheat from frozen in a saucepan, stirring all the time. Add 2 tablespoons milk if the soup is too thick.


## Kidney soup

### Makes 6–8 portions

METRIC/IMPERIAL
2 tablespoons oil
1 large onion, chopped
225 g/8 oz ox kidney
2 beef stock cubes
generous 1 litre/2 pints water
2 tablespoons tomato purée

1 teaspoon sugar
¼ teaspoon ground cloves
1 bouquet garni
25 g/1 oz butter
25 g/1 oz flour
4 tablespoons dry sherry
salt and black pepper

1 Heat the oil and use to fry the onion gently until soft.
2 Trim the kidney and cut into small pieces. Add to the pan and fry briskly until browned. Add the crumbled stock cubes, water, tomato purée, sugar, spice and bouquet garni and bring to the boil, stirring constantly. Cover and simmer for about 1 hour, or until the kidney is tender. Discard the bouquet garni.
3 In a clean saucepan, melt the butter and stir in the flour. Cook for 2 minutes. Gradually add the kidney mixture and bring to the boil, stirring constantly. Cook for 3 minutes, stir in the sherry and season to taste.
4 Liquidise the soup before freezing.
5 Reheat from frozen in a saucepan, stirring frequently.

# Sauces

## Gardener's curry sauce

### Makes 4 portions

METRIC/IMPERIAL

| | |
|---|---|
| 225 g/8 oz lentils | I tablespoon curry |
| 2 chicken stock cubes | powder |
| 900 ml/1½ pints boiling | 2 tablespoons oil |
| water | 2 large onions, chopped |
| I large carrot, chopped | 4 medium tomatoes, |
| I medium parsnip, | chopped |
| chopped | 2 cloves of garlic, |
| I tablespoon desiccated | chopped |
| coconut | salt |

1 Soak the lentils in cold water to cover overnight. Drain.
2 Dissolve the stock cubes in the boiling water. Add the lentils, carrot, parsnip, coconut and curry powder.
3 Bring to the boil, cover and simmer for 1 hour, or until the mixture is thick.
4 Heat half the oil and use to fry the onion gently until soft. Add the remaining oil, tomato and garlic and cook for a further 5 minutes.
5 Combine the two mixtures and bring to the boil stirring constantly. Simmer for 2 minutes.
6 Add salt to taste before freezing in a polythene container.
7 Reheat from frozen in a saucepan, stirring frequently. Add a little water if the mixture is too thick. Serve with boiled rice.

## Piquant tomato sauce

### Makes about I litre/1¾ pints

METRIC/IMPERIAL

| | |
|---|---|
| I kg/2 lb ripe tomatoes, | 2 canned red pimentos, |
| peeled | chopped |
| 2 medium onions, | I teaspoon dried thyme |
| chopped | I teaspoon dried oregano |
| 2 tablespoons oil | I tablespoon |
| 25 g/I oz cornflour | Worcestershire sauce |
| 300 ml/½ pint water | salt and pepper |

1 Chop the tomatoes and cook gently with the onion in the oil until soft.
2 Moisten the cornflour with a little of the water and add to the tomato mixture. Stir constantly over gentle heat for 2 minutes.
3 Add the remaining water together with the pimento, thyme, oregano, Worcestershire sauce and seasoning to taste. Bring to the boil, stirring all the time. Cook for 5 minutes.
4 Liquidise the mixture before freezing in polythene containers.
5 Reheat from frozen in a saucepan, stirring frequently.

## Basic barbecue sauce

### Makes about 900 ml/1½ pints

METRIC/IMPERIAL

| | |
|---|---|
| I large red pepper, | 3 tablespoons tomato |
| deseeded | purée |
| 3 cloves garlic | 1½ teaspoons |
| 4 tablespoons oil | Worcestershire sauce |
| I medium onion, grated | 100 g/4 oz soft brown |
| 2 tablespoons cornflour | sugar |
| 450 ml/¾ pint water | salt and pepper |
| 4 tablespoons white | |
| vinegar | |

1 Very finely chop the pepper and garlic. Heat the oil and use to fry the pepper, garlic and onion gently until soft but not browned. Sprinkle in the cornflour and stir well. Gradually add the water and vinegar and bring to the boil, stirring constantly. Add the tomato purée, sugar and Worcestershire sauce and stir until the sugar has dissolved.
2 Bring back to the boil and simmer for 5 minutes, stirring frequently. Season to taste.
3 Liquidise before freezing if you prefer a completely smooth sauce. Freeze in polythene containers.
4 Turn still frozen into a saucepan, add 2 tablespoons water and reheat gently to boiling point, stirring frequently.

## Chocolate sauce

### Makes 4 portions

METRIC/IMPERIAL

| | |
|---|---|
| 100 g/4 oz plain chocolate | 2 teaspoons vanilla |
| 25 g/I oz butter | essence |
| 2 tablespoons milk | |

1 Break up the chocolate and place in a double boiler or basin over a pan of hot water. Add the butter and allow to melt. Stir well and gradually add the milk and vanilla essence. Remove from the heat as soon as the sauce is smooth.
2 Freeze in a small boiling bag.
3 Reheat the frozen bag in a pan of boiling water for about 10 minutes. Snip off a corner of the bag and press out the sauce. If served cold, stir the sauce briskly when defrosted.

### Variations:

**Mocha sauce:** Use only 1 teaspoon vanilla essence and add 2 teaspoons coffee essence when adding the milk.

**Chocolate and orange sauce:** Substitute 3 tablespoons orange juice for the milk and vanilla essence and beat the finely grated zest of 1 orange into the sauce when it is removed from the heat.

**Peppermint chocolate sauce:** Substitute 150 g/5 oz chocolate peppermint creams for the chocolate and omit the vanilla essence.

**Chocolate and rum sauce:** Substitute 2 teaspoons rum for the vanilla essence.

**Nutty chocolate sauce:** Stir 50 g/2 oz chopped mixed nuts into the sauce before freezing.

# Smooth butterscotch sauce

## Makes 6–8 portions

METRIC/IMPERIAL

| | |
|---|---|
| 50 g/2 oz butter | pinch of salt |
| 75 g/3 oz demerara sugar | 100 ml/4 fl oz evaporated |
| 50 g/2 oz granulated | milk |
| sugar | ½ teaspoon vanilla |
| 175 g/6 oz golden syrup | essence |

1 Melt the butter in a saucepan, add the sugars, syrup and salt and stir well. Heat gently, stirring very frequently, until the mixture comes to the boil. Reduce the heat and allow to boil gently for about 20 minutes, stirring now and then, until the sauce is a rich golden brown. Cool, stirring occasionally.
2 Gradually beat in the evaporated milk and vanilla essence until the mixture is well blended.
3 Freeze in polythene containers.
4 Defrost, stir briskly and serve cold.

### Variations:
**Rich butterscotch sauce:** Substitute 100 ml/4 fl oz double cream for the evaporated milk. Defrost in the refrigerator.

**Lemon butterscotch sauce:** Add the finely grated rind of 1 lemon and 1 teaspoon lemon juice to the sauce before it cools. Omit the vanilla essence.

# Simplicity sauces

Good basic sauces can be made by the one-stage method where all the ingredients go into the saucepan together. This is a thick coating sauce; to use as a pouring sauce add 150 ml/¼ pint extra milk.

# Savoury white sauce

## Makes generous 1 litre/2 pints

METRIC/IMPERIAL

| | |
|---|---|
| 100 g/4 oz butter | 2 chicken stock cubes, |
| 100 g/4 oz flour | crumbled |
| generous 1 litre/2 pints milk | |

1 Place all the ingredients in a large saucepan and whisk steadily over moderate heat until the sauce comes to the boil. Reduce the heat and simmer for a further 2 minutes, whisking all the time.
2 Pour into polythene containers and lay a sheet of cling film over the surface of the sauce before freezing.

3 Defrost and then reheat in a saucepan over gentle heat, stirring all the time. If reheating from frozen, add 2 tablespoons milk to help prevent the sauce from burning.

### Variations:
To flavour 300 ml/½ pint sauce.

**Parsley sauce:** Stir 1–2 tablespoons chopped parsley into the sauce as it reheats. To serve with fish, add 1 tablespoon vinegar or 1 teaspoon lemon juice. To serve with chicken or other delicately flavoured meat, add a good pinch of ground nutmeg.

**Cheese sauce:** Stir 1 teaspoon mustard and 100 g/4 oz grated hard cheese into the sauce when it has reheated to boiling point. Remove from the heat as soon as the sauce is smooth again.

**Piquant white sauce:** Stir 1 teaspoon chopped gherkins, 1 teaspoon chopped capers and 1 teaspoon liquid from each jar into the sauce as it reheats.

**Enriched sauces:** All the above sauces can be enriched by beating in an egg yolk off the heat when the sauce has been reheated ready to serve.

# All-purpose pickling syrup

This syrup can be defrosted and used as a poaching liquid for fruit to serve as a savoury accompaniment to main dishes or fruit can be poached in it and frozen in it to serve cold as an alternative to chutney. Suitable fruits are halved and stoned plums, peeled, quartered and cored pears, peeled, stoned and halved peaches.

## Makes about 600 ml/1 pint

METRIC/IMPERIAL

| | |
|---|---|
| 150 ml/¼ pint water | 1 tablespoon mixed |
| 300 ml/½ pint wine | pickling spices |
| vinegar | 5-cm/2-inch length |
| 175 g/6 oz soft brown | cinnamon stick |
| sugar | 4 tablespoons redcurrant |
| 225 g/8 oz granulated | jelly |
| sugar | |

1 Place the water, vinegar and sugars in a saucepan and heat gently, stirring until dissolved. Add the pickling spices, cinnamon stick and redcurrant jelly and stir over heat until the jelly has melted. Bring to the boil and simmer for 4 minutes.

### Variations:
**Blackcurrant pickling syrup:** Substitute blackcurrant jelly for the redcurrant jelly and use 4 cloves instead of the cinnamon stick.

**Blackberry pickling syrup:** Substitute bramble jelly for the redcurrant jelly and use 2 blades of mace instead of the cinnamon stick.

**Cranberry pickling syrup:** Substitute cranberry sauce for the redcurrant jelly.

# Pâtés and terrines

## Woodland pâté

**Makes 8 portions**

METRIC/IMPERIAL
150 ml/¼ pint vinegar
4 tablespoons dry sherry
4 tablespoons beef stock
½ teaspoon dried
  marjoram
½ teaspoon dried thyme
5 black peppercorns

I bay leaf
salt
3 pigeons, jointed
I thick slice brown bread
175 g/6 oz pork
  sausagemeat

1 Mix together the vinegar, sherry, stock, marjoram, thyme, peppercorns, bay leaf and add a little seasoning. Use to marinate the pigeon portions for about 2 days in the refrigerator in a covered container.
2 Soak the bread in the marinade for 2 minutes, then drain pigeon and bread.
3 Remove the pigeon flesh from the bones and mix with the sausagemeat and soaked bread. Add salt to taste, mix together thoroughly.
4 Press the mixture into a greased 1-kg/2-lb loaf tin, cover and stand in a roasting tin half-filled with water. Cook in a moderate oven (180°C, 350°F, Gas Mark 4) for 1½ hours.
5 Chill, then remove from the tin if necessary before freezing. Wrap whole pâté in foil or slice before freezing.

## Tarragon-topped pâté

**Makes 6–8 portions**

METRIC/IMPERIAL
50 g/2 oz margarine
I medium onion, chopped
100 g/4 oz fat bacon,
  derinded
0·75 kg/1½ lb chicken
  livers
2 eggs, beaten

I teaspoon ground mixed
  spice
salt and pepper
fresh tarragon leaves
150 ml/¼ pint double
  strength aspic jelly

1 Melt the margarine and use to cook the onion until soft. Chop the bacon and chicken livers, add to the pan and cook for 3 minutes.
2 Liquidise, stir in the eggs, spice and seasoning to taste.
3 Press the mixture into a greased ovenproof dish. Cover and place in a roasting tin half-filled with water. Cook in a moderate oven (180°C, 350°F, Gas Mark 4) for 45 minutes.
4 Arrange the tarragon leaves on top and pour over the aspic jelly.
5 Chill until jelly is set before freezing.

## Party pâté

**Makes 8 portions**

METRIC/IMPERIAL
2 tablespoons oil
I large onion, chopped
50 g/2 oz bacon, derinded
175 g/6 oz pigs' liver,
  sliced
175 g/6 oz cooked duck
  or turkey, diced

100 g/4 oz sausagemeat
I tablespoon lemon juice
I egg, beaten
2 tablespoons dry cider
  or apple juice
salt and pepper
4 bay leaves

1 Heat the oil and use to cook the onion, bacon and liver until slightly browned.
2 Mince the mixture with the duck or turkey, sausagemeat, lemon juice, egg, cider or apple juice and seasoning to taste.
3 Press the mixture into a greased 450-g/1-lb loaf tin and place the bay leaves on top. Cook in a moderate oven (180°C, 350°F, Gas Mark 4) for 45 minutes.
4 Chill, remove from the tin if necessary and freeze whole or in slices.

## Spiced chicken liver pâté

**Makes 4 portions**

METRIC/IMPERIAL
450 g/1 lb chicken livers
225 g/8 oz butter
I teaspoon
  Worcestershire sauce
2 teaspoons dry mustard

½ teaspoon ground mace
½ teaspoon ground
  allspice
I medium onion, grated
salt and pepper

1 Place the livers in a saucepan and just cover with water. Poach gently for about 25 minutes, until tender. Drain very well and liquidise with 50 g/2 oz of the butter and the Worcestershire sauce until smooth. Cool.
2 Beat the remaining butter until soft and gradually beat in the flavourings and onion. Add the liver mixture and beat until the mixture is well blended. Season to taste.
3 Press into a foil container before freezing.
4 Defrost in the refrigerator.

## Terrine of pork

**Makes 6–8 portions**

METRIC/IMPERIAL
I tablespoon oil
275 g/10 oz pigs' liver
I large onion
3 cloves garlic
175 g/6 oz pork
  sausagemeat
450 g/1 lb minced pork

50 g/2 oz soft
  breadcrumbs
I teaspoon dried sage
salt and pepper
175 g/6 oz streaky bacon,
  derinded
I bay leaf

1 Heat the oil and use to fry the slices of liver briefly on each side until just firm. Mince finely.
2 Very finely chop the onion and garlic and mix with the liver, sausagemeat, pork, breadcrumbs, herbs and seasoning to taste.

3 Line a foil container with the rashers of bacon and fill with the liver mixture. Press down well and fold the ends of the bacon rashers over the mixture. Place the bay leaf on top.
4 Cover the container with foil and stand it in a roasting tin. Pour in water to a depth of 2·5 cm/1 inch and cook in a cool oven (150°C, 300°F, Gas Mark 2) for about 2 hours. Remove the bay leaf.
5 Weight the top and chill before freezing.
6 Defrost at room temperature then turn out before serving.

### Variation:
Terrine of veal: Substitute minced veal for the pork, use lambs' liver instead of the pigs' liver and marjoram or oregano for the sage.

## Terrine of game

### Makes 6–8 portions
METRIC/IMPERIAL

| | |
|---|---|
| 2 large joints rabbit | ½ teaspoon dried sage |
| 2 large joints hare | ¼ teaspoon ground cloves |
| 225 g/8 oz piece of streaky bacon, derinded | 300 ml/½ pint beef stock |
| 2 cloves garlic, crushed | 300 ml/½ pint robust red wine |
| 1 large onion, sliced | salt and pepper |
| 2 bay leaves | 100 g/4 oz streaky bacon rashers, derinded |
| 1 teaspoon dried marjoram | |

1 Place the rabbit and hare in a saucepan and add the piece of bacon, the garlic, onion, bay leaves, herbs, spice and seasoning. Pour over the stock and wine and bring to the boil. Cover and simmer for about 1¼ hours, or until the meat is tender.
2 Remove the flesh from the bones and strain the liquid. Liquidise or mince the meat with sufficient of the reserved liquid to make a soft paste.
3 Stretch the bacon rashers and use to line a large foil container. Fill with the game mixture and fold over the ends of the bacon rashers. Pour in as much of the reserved liquid as possible.
4 Place the container in a roasting tin and pour in water to a depth of 2·5 cm/1 inch. Cook in a very cool oven (120°C, 250°F, Gas Mark ½) for about 1½ hours.
5 Cover with foil before freezing.
6 Defrost in the refrigerator and turn out before serving.

# Mousses and pots

## Ham cream mousse

### Makes 4 portions
METRIC/IMPERIAL

| | |
|---|---|
| 2 teaspoons gelatine | pinch of paprika pepper |
| 2 tablespoons water | 2 eggs, separated |
| 225 g/8 oz lean ham | 150 ml/¼ pint double cream |
| 1 tablespoon tomato ketchup | salt and pepper |

1 Dissolve the gelatine in the water in a basin over hot water. Cool.
2 Liquidise the ham with the ketchup, paprika and egg yolks until smooth.
3 Lightly whip the cream and fold into the ham mixture with the dissolved gelatine and seasoning to taste.
4 When the ham mixture begins to thicken, whip the egg whites until stiff and fold in lightly. Turn into a rinsed ring mould and chill until set.
5 Freeze in the mould.
6 Dip the mould in warm water and turn the frozen mousse out on a serving dish. Defrost in the refrigerator and serve cold.

### Variations:
Chicken cream mousse: Substitute 225 g/8 oz cooked chicken for the ham and add a few drops of Tabasco with the tomato ketchup.

Salmon cream mousse: Substitute a drained, boned and flaked 198-g/7-oz can of pink salmon for the ham and use 1 tablespoon salad cream instead of the tomato ketchup.

## Smoked mackerel mousse

### Makes 8 portions
METRIC/IMPERIAL

| | |
|---|---|
| 1 tablespoon gelatine | 2 eggs, separated |
| 2 tablespoons water | 4 tablespoons salad cream |
| 350 g/12 oz smoked mackerel | 2 teaspoons lemon juice |
| 50 g/2 oz butter | salt and black pepper |
| 1 teaspoon Worcestershire sauce | |

1 Dissolve the gelatine in the water in a basin over a pan of hot water. Cool.
2 Remove all skin and bone from the mackerel and flake or chop. Melt the butter, stir in the mackerel and sprinkle in the Worcestershire sauce. Heat through, stirring, and divide between 8 individual dishes.
3 Whip the egg yolks, add the salad cream and lemon juice and continue beating until smooth. Stir in the dissolved gelatine.
4 When the mixture thickens, whisk the cream and egg whites separately and fold these into the egg mixture. Season to taste, divide between the dishes and allow to set.

**5** Open freeze before covering.

**6** Uncover while frozen and allow to defrost at room temperature.

**Variations:**
**Smoked whiting mousse:** Substitute 350 g/12 oz smoked whiting fillet for the smoked mackerel.

**Kipper mousse:** Substitute 350 g/12 oz kipper fillets for the smoked mackerel and poach them before making the mousse. Season with pepper and add salt only if necessary.

**Smoked salmon mousse:** Substitute 350 g/12 oz smoked salmon pieces for the smoked mackerel.

## Creamy ham and apple moulds

### Makes 6 portions
METRIC/IMPERIAL

| | |
|---|---|
| 300 ml/½ pint Savoury white sauce (see page 60) | 150 ml/¼ pint apple purée |
| 3 tablespoons mayonnaise | 100 g/4 oz ham, chopped |
| 2 tablespoons lemon juice | salt and pepper |
| 1 tablespoon gelatine | 150 ml/¼ pint double cream |
| 2 tablespoons water | |

**1** Beat together the sauce, mayonnaise and lemon juice. Dissolve the gelatine in the water in a basin over hot water. Cool and stir into the sauce mixture with the apple purée and ham. Add seasoning to taste.

**2** When the mixture thickens, whip the cream and fold in lightly. Divide between 6 individual moulds and allow to set.

**3** Freeze in the moulds.

**4** Dip the frozen moulds in warm water and turn out on a serving dish. Cover and allow to defrost at room temperature.

**Variation:**
**Creamy shellfish and apple moulds:** Substitute 100 g/4 oz chopped prawns, shrimps or crabmeat for the ham.

## Smoked fish mousse

### Makes 6–8 portions
METRIC/IMPERIAL

| | |
|---|---|
| 225 g/8 oz smoked cod or haddock fillet | 150 ml/¼ pint chicken stock |
| about 450 ml/¾ pint milk | 150 ml/¼ pint mayonnaise |
| 40 g/1½ oz butter | salt and pepper |
| 40 g/1½ oz flour | 300 ml/½ pint double cream |
| 1 tablespoon gelatine | |

**1** Place the fish in a saucepan and cover with water. Bring to boiling point and drain. Pour over the milk and poach gently for about 10 minutes, until the fish flakes easily. Lift out the fish, remove any skin and bones and flake. Strain the cooking liquid and make it up to 450 ml/¾ pint again with more milk if necessary.

**2** Melt the butter and stir in the flour. Cook for 1 minute. Gradually add the strained liquid and bring to the boil, stirring constantly. Cool.

**3** Dissolve the gelatine in the stock in a basin over hot water. Cool.

**4** Mix together the cooled sauce, mayonnaise and dissolved gelatine until smooth. Stir in the fish and season to taste with pepper and a little salt if necessary. When the mixture begins to thicken, fold in the cream. Turn into a 15–17·5-cm/6–7-inch soufflé dish and allow to set.

**5** Cover the dish with foil or cling film before freezing.

**6** Uncover and defrost at room temperature.

## Schooner pots

### Makes 4 portions
METRIC/IMPERIAL

| | |
|---|---|
| 25 g/1 oz butter | 4 tablespoons dry sherry |
| 225 g/8 oz Cheddar cheese, grated | 16 walnut halves |
| ½ teaspoon ground mace or ¼ teaspoon ground cloves | |

**1** Cream the butter and gradually beat in the cheese, spice and sherry.

**2** Divide the mixture into 4 equal portions and press into individual pots. Arrange 4 walnut halves on each pot, pressing them well into the mixture.

**3** Cover the pots with foil or cling film before freezing.

**4** Defrost and serve at room temperature.

## Potted prawns

### Makes 4 portions
METRIC/IMPERIAL

| | |
|---|---|
| 175 g/6 oz peeled prawns, chopped | pinch of cayenne pepper |
| 100 g/4 oz butter | 1 teaspoon ground black pepper |
| 2 tablespoons lemon juice | 1 teaspoon ground mace |

**1** Chop the prawns roughly and place in a saucepan with 25 g/1 oz of the butter, the lemon juice, cayenne, black pepper and mace. Heat gently until the butter melts and the prawns are heated through.

**2** Divide the mixture among 4 ramekin dishes and press down. Melt the remaining butter and pour over the prawn mixture in the pots.

**3** Chill and then cover with foil before freezing.

**4** Defrost in the refrigerator and serve cold.

**Variation:**
**Potted crab:** Substitute 175 g/6 oz crabmeat for the prawns and use ¾ teaspoon ground nutmeg instead of the mace.

## French cheese pots

**Makes 4 portions**

METRIC/IMPERIAL

| | |
|---|---|
| I ripe whole Camembert cheese | 3 tablespoons soured cream |
| 75 g/3 oz cream cheese | ½ teaspoon dry mustard |
| 2 tablespoons hot milk | salt and pepper |

1 Remove the soft crust from the Camembert with a sharp knife. Mix with the cream cheese and beat until smooth or pound the mixture in a mortar.
2 Beat in the milk, soured cream, dry mustard and seasoning to taste. Continue beating until smooth.
3 Pack the mixture in individual containers before freezing.
4 Defrost and serve with crisp French bread.


## Liver and egg pots

**Makes 4–6 portions**

METRIC/IMPERIAL

| | |
|---|---|
| 50 g/2 oz butter | I teaspoon salt |
| I small onion, grated | I tablespoon single cream |
| 225 g/8 oz chicken livers | 2 hard-boiled eggs, sliced |
| 2 tablespoons fresh brown breadcrumbs | pepper |

1 Melt the butter and use to fry the onion gently until soft. Add the livers and cook for about 5 minutes, until firm but still pink in the centres.
2 Place the contents of the pan in a blender and add the breadcrumbs, salt, cream and hard-boiled eggs. Liquidise until smooth and add pepper to taste.
3 Pack in polythene containers for freezing.
4 Defrost at room temperature and serve with hot toast or as a spread.

### Variations:

**Herbed liver and egg pots:** Add 2 tablespoons chopped fresh herbs when liquidising the liver mixture. Season with garlic salt.

**Liver and mushroom pots:** Slice 75 g/3 oz button mushrooms and fry with the onion in the butter. Omit the hard-boiled eggs.


# Starters

## Cold courgette starter

**Makes 8 portions**

METRIC/IMPERIAL

| | |
|---|---|
| 2 large slices white bread | 3 tablespoons lemon juice |
| 4 tablespoons oil | 2 chicken stock cubes |
| 150 ml/¼ pint unsweetened orange juice | 2 large onions, grated |
| | 0·75 kg/1½ lb courgettes |
| | 50 g/2 oz salami, sliced |

1 Trim crusts from bread, cut into small dice. Fry until golden in half the oil. Drain and cool on absorbent paper.
2 Place the remaining oil, fruit juices and stock cubes in a large saucepan and heat until the cubes have dissolved. Add the onion and simmer for 5 minutes.
3 Top and tail the courgettes and slice them thinly. Add to the pan, bring back to the boil, cover and simmer until tender. Cool. Chop the salami and stir into the courgette mixture.
4 Freeze the croûtons in two small polythene containers and the courgette mixture in two larger polythene containers.
5 Defrost courgette mixture, divide between small glass dishes, sprinkle with defrosted croûtons.


## Hors d'oeuvres fillings

The following mixtures are suitable to fill hollowed out 'cups' made from short lengths of cucumber, scooped out tomatoes, scraped out lemon halves, or lengths of celery. Freeze in polythene containers and defrost well before spooning into the prepared 'cup'.

**Tuna filling:** Combine 100 g/4 oz drained and flaked canned tuna, 1 tablespoon chopped sweet brown pickle and 1 tablespoon lemon juice. Season with onion salt and pepper to taste. When serving, garnish the filling with snipped mustard and cress.

**Liver sausage filling:** Mash 100 g/4 oz Continental liver sausage and combine with 4 tablespoons soured cream, 1 teaspoon Worcestershire and a few drops of Tabasco. Derind and grill 2 rashers streaky bacon until crisp. Crumble and fold into the liver sausage mixture before freezing. When serving, garnish the filling with finely chopped hard-boiled egg.

**Sherried mushroom filling:** Place 100 g/4 oz finely sliced button mushrooms in a polythene container and pour over 2 tablespoons dry sherry. Cover and chill for about 4 hours, turning the container once during this time. Beat 50 g/2 oz cream cheese until smooth and gradually mix in the mushroom mixture and 1 tablespoon salad cream. When serving, garnish the filling with sliced stuffed green olives.

# Flavoured butters and dips

## Flavoured butters

The following butters are easy to make provided that the butter is softened beforehand. The same recipes could also be made with margarine, but in this case soft margarines are not suitable as they melt too quickly on defrosting.

**Makes about 225 g/8 oz flavoured butter**
The flavouring should be beaten or pounded into the softened butter until the mixture is well blended, chilled, then formed into a roll about 2·5 cm/1 inch in diameter and wrapped closely in freezer tissue or foil. Slices can be cut from the frozen roll as required. These variations are to flavour 225 g/8 oz of butter.

**Lemon butter:** Gradually incorporate 2 teaspoons finely grated lemon rind and 4 tablespoons lemon juice.

**Cheese butter:** Beat in 100 g/4 oz cream or curd cheese and 100 g/4 oz finely grated hard cheese. Add seasoning of salt, pepper and mustard to taste.

**Anchovy butter:** Drain and pound the fillets from a 50-g/2-oz can of anchovies with 1 teaspoon lemon juice. Gradually add the softened butter and season with black pepper.

**Curry butter:** Beat in 1 teaspoon curry powder and 1 teaspoon lemon juice.

**Green savoury butter:** Sieve 4 tablespoons well drained spinach purée and beat into the butter with ½ teaspoon anchovy essence.

**Crab butter:** Beat in the contents of a 45-g/1¾-oz can of dressed crab.

**Pimento butter:** Well drain and pound 1 large canned red pimento with 1 teaspoon tomato ketchup. Gradually add the softened butter and season with black pepper.

**Garlic butter:** Beat in ¾–1 teaspoon pure garlic powder and salt and pepper to taste.

**Worcestershire butter:** Beat in 1 teaspoon Worcestershire sauce.

**Fresh herb butters:** While they are in season, mixed herb butters or those flavoured with a single herb of your choice are easy to make and keep well until the time of year when only dried herbs are available. Allow 3 tablespoons finely chopped fresh herbs to 225 g/8 oz butter. Mint, parsley, chives, marjoram, tarragon, oregano and thyme are suitable. Sage and rosemary are less successful.

**Gourmet herb pats:** The flavour of the herbs is intensified by the addition of ½–1 teaspoon Brandy pounded with 1 teaspoon fine dry breadcrumbs and incorporated with the herbs.

**Sweet butters:** To serve with baked or steamed puddings, baked apples or fruit pies.

**Spiced butters:** It is useful to be able to produce these butters from your freezer as an alternative to custard or whipped cream. Allow 1 tablespoon clear honey and 1–2 teaspoons ground spice according to the strength of the spice with 225 g/8 oz butter.

**Fruit butters:** These can be made with lemon, orange or lime flavouring using unsalted butter. Allow 2 tablespoons castor or icing sugar per 225 g/8 oz butter and grated rind and juice of the fruit in proportion as given for Lemon butter above.

## Sardine and tomato dip

### Makes 4 portions

METRIC/IMPERIAL

| | |
|---|---|
| 100-g/4-oz can sardines in tomato sauce | 1 tablespoon grated onion |
| 75 g/3 oz cream cheese | 2 teaspoons Worcestershire sauce |
| 1 tablespoon lemon juice | garlic salt and pepper |

1 Mash the sardines with the sauce from the can until smooth.
2 In a separate bowl, beat the cream cheese until soft and gradually add the sardine mixture, lemon juice, onion and Worcestershire sauce. Season to taste with garlic salt and pepper.
3 Freeze in a polythene container.
4 Defrost and then beat well before serving.

## Avocado and crab dip

### Makes 4 portions

METRIC/IMPERIAL

| | |
|---|---|
| 1 large avocado | 42-g/1½-oz can dressed crab |
| 1 tablespoon lemon juice | salt and pepper |
| 2 tablespoons mayonnaise | 6 stuffed olives green |
| 75 g/3 oz cream cheese | |

1 Peel the avocado, halve and remove the stone. Mash the flesh with the lemon juice and mayonnaise. Beat in the cream cheese.
2 Blend the cheese mixture with the crab and season to taste.
3 Roughly chop the olives and fold into the mixture.
4 Freeze in a polythene container.
5 Defrost at room temperature and stir with a fork before serving.

**Hint:**
Dips can be piled into a small dish, placed in the centre of a large plate and surrounded with biscuits or crisps to use as dippers.

# Pack-away pastry

Pastry making for the freezer can be a very flexible art because you have a number of choices. First, you can make all the pastry yourself or choose to make only the easier kinds. In this book I have recommended using bought frozen puff pastry and making flaky pastry from a packet mix. Shortcrust is so simple that most housewives prefer to make it themselves but this also can be bought ready made in a frozen form and in a packet mix. You may like to prepare large quantities of pastry and freeze it in convenient-sized portions to use as required. It needs to be closely wrapped in foil or strong cling wrap to prevent it forming a skin. You must allow time for defrosting but it does save the bother of pastry-making when you want to make just a flan or tart.

### Freezing baked or unbaked?

There is a good case for freezing most pastry dishes without actually baking them, even though they may contain cooked fillings. The length of time it takes in the oven to defrost and bake is very little longer than to defrost and reheat. Both methods have been suggested but if you really prefer the alternative way, just remember that such items as fresh fruit may be over-cooked if you fully bake a fruit tart before freezing and then decide to defrost and reheat in the oven. Cooked pastry, especially unfilled pastry cases, is very fragile and needs the protection of a rigid container in the freezer. Many disasters are saved by baking flans in rings on ovenproof plates, or turning out cooked flans on to serving plates, even if it means inverting a rigid 'protector' over the base for freezing. Filled pastry flans are less liable to be damaged if handled while they are frozen if, for example, it is necessary to transfer from one container to another or decorate. Piped decorations also tend to get spoiled by careless handling and for this reason they have not been suggested in this chapter but you can improve the appearance of open flans and tarts at serving time by adding decorations then.

### Choux pastry problems

There are different schools of thought on the best way to handle choux pastry. Cooked puffs filled and packed in layers in rigid-based containers are ready to serve but the puffs lack some of the crispness you can obtain by popping them for a brief sojourn in the oven, something you cannot do if they are filled with, for example, flavoured whipped cream. Since making choux paste is a rather more elaborate process than the rubbed-in mix, you might prefer to make it up and freeze it uncooked. As with preparing shortcrust pastry, the basic paste may require a couple of hours to defrost but there is no mess involved. You can take this one stage further. Pipe out puffs on baking sheets, open freeze and then pack in containers. But do arrange them quickly well apart on greased baking sheets and get them into the oven while still fully frozen. Depending on size they will require an extra 5–7 minutes at baking time.

# Shortcrust pastry

## Herby salad flan

**Makes 4–6 portions**

METRIC/IMPERIAL
*shortcrust pastry*::
175 g/6 oz plain flour
pinch of salt
40 g/1½ oz lard

40 g/1½ oz margarine
about 2 tablespoons cold
   water

*filling:*
2 eggs, beaten
1 teaspoon dried mixed
   herbs
2 tablespoons cottage
   cheese
75 g/3 oz Cheddar cheese,
   grated

1 tablespoon corn oil
50 g/2 oz chopped parsley
salt and pepper
2 medium tomatoes,
   sliced

1 Sift the flour and salt into a bowl and rub in the fats. Add sufficient water to make a firm dough. Roll out and use to line a greased 20-cm/8-inch foil flan case.
2 Beat together the egg, dried herbs, cottage cheese, most of the grated cheese, the corn oil and parsley. Season to taste.
3 Arrange the tomato slices in the pastry case, add the cheese mixture and top with the remaining grated cheese.
4 Bake in a moderate oven (180°C, 350°F, Gas Mark 4) for about 45 minutes.
5 Open freeze before covering.
6 Defrost and serve cold, or reheat from frozen in a moderately hot oven (200°C, 400°F, Gas Mark 6) for about 20 minutes.

### Variations:

**Ham and egg flan:** Substitute a filling made by frying 1 medium chopped onion in 25 g/1 oz butter until soft. Stir in 100 g/4 oz finely chopped ham then spoon into the pastry case. Beat 2 eggs into 300 ml/½ pint milk with 2 tablespoons finely chopped parsley and seasoning to taste. Pour over the ham mixture and bake as above.

**Smoked mackerel flan:** Use the filling recipe for Ham and egg flan but substitute 100 g/4 oz flaked smoked mackerel fillet for the ham and season generously with black pepper.

**Spinach flan:** Substitute a filling made by mixing 225 g/8 oz cooked puréed spinach with 25 g/1 oz melted butter, 225 g/8 oz cottage cheese, 2 beaten eggs, 2 tablespoons evaporated milk, ½ teaspoon ground nutmeg and seasoning to taste. Pour into the pastry case, sprinkle with 25 g/1 oz grated Cheddar cheese and bake as above.

## Lemon chicken double crust pie

**Makes 4–6 portions**

METRIC/IMPERIAL
*pastry:*
225 g/8 oz plain flour
¼ teaspoon salt
150 g/5 oz butter

3–4 tablespoons cold
   water

*filling:*
40 g/1½ oz butter
1 small onion, chopped
40 g/1½ oz flour
150 ml/¼ pint chicken
   stock
300 ml/½ pint milk
grated rind and juice of
   1 lemon

1 teaspoon chopped
   parsley
salt and pepper
450 g/1 lb cooked
   chicken

1 To make the pastry, sift the flour and salt into a bowl and rub in the butter. Add sufficient cold water to make a stiff dough. Chill while you make the filling.
2 Melt the butter and use to fry the onion gently until soft. Stir in the flour and gradually add the stock and milk. Bring to the boil stirring constantly. Add the lemon rind and juice and the parsley and season to taste. Cut the chicken into strips and fold into the sauce. Cool.
3 Roll out half the pastry and use to line a 20-cm/8-inch foil flan case or 2·5-cm/1-inch deep pie plate. Fill with the chicken mixture. Roll out remaining pastry to form a lid. Dampen the edges and seal well together. Decorate with pastry trimmings.
4 Bake in a moderately hot oven (200°C, 400°F, Gas Mark 6) for 30 minutes.
5 Open freeze then cover with foil before freezing.
6 Reheat from frozen still covered, in a moderately hot oven (200°C, 400°F, Gas Mark 6) for 35 minutes. Remove foil and return to the oven for a further 10 minutes.

### Variations:

**Cornish rabbit pie:** Substitute 350 g/12 oz cooked rabbit and 100 g/4 oz cooked diced swede for the chicken and use 3 tablespoons milk in place of the lemon rind and juice. Season generously with salt and black pepper.

**Coley and corn pie:** Substitute 350 g/12 oz cooked flaked coley, 1 very finely chopped hard boiled egg and 75 g/3 oz cooked or canned sweetcorn kernels for the chicken.

## Savoury pork pasties

**Makes 6 pasties**

METRIC/IMPERIAL
350 g/12 oz shortcrust
   pastry (see page 67)
50 g/2 oz sage and onion
   stuffing mix
1 tablespoon mango
   chutney, chopped
4 tablespoons boiling
   water

225 g/8 oz cooked lean
   pork, diced
100-g/4-oz can sweetcorn
   kernels, drained
1 egg, beaten

1 Roll out the pastry and use to cut six 15-cm/6-inch circles.
2 Mix together the stuffing mix, chutney and boiling water. Fold in the pork and sweetcorn.
3 Divide the filling between the pastry circles, fold over and seal the edges with beaten egg. Prick each pasty once with a fork, place on a greased baking sheet and brush all over with beaten egg.
4 Bake in a moderately hot oven (200°C, 400°F, Gas Mark 6) for about 25 minutes, until well-risen and golden brown.
5 Pack in layers with dividers for freezing.
6 Defrost and serve cold. If required hot, reheat from frozen in a moderately hot oven as above for 20 minutes.

## Neapolitan quiche

### Makes 4–6 portions

METRIC/IMPERIAL

6 canned anchovy fillets
175 g/6 oz shortcrust pastry (see page 67)
450 g/1 lb ripe tomatoes, peeled
½ teaspoon chopped basil or pinch of dried basil
50 g/2 oz Cheddar cheese, grated

25 g/1 oz butter
1 small onion, chopped
2 eggs
300 ml/½ pint milk
salt and pepper
6 stuffed green olives, halved

1 Drain the anchovy fillets and dry on absorbent paper.
2 Roll out the pastry and use to line a 20-cm/8-inch foil flan case.
3 Deseed and roughly chop the tomatoes, place in the pastry case and sprinkle with the basil and grated cheese.
4 Melt the butter and use to fry the onion gently until soft. Add to the pastry case.
5 Beat the eggs with the milk and salt and pepper to taste and pour into the flan.
6 Arrange the anchovy fillets and olives on top and bake in a moderately hot oven (190°C, 375°F, Gas Mark 5) for 25–30 minutes until golden brown.
7 Open freeze then cover with foil.
8 Reheat from frozen still covered in a moderately hot oven (200°C, 400°F, Gas Mark 6) for 25 minutes. Remove foil and return to the oven for a further 10 minutes.

## Cheese pastry tartlet or flan

### Makes 18 tartlet cases, or 2 20-cm/8-inch flan cases

METRIC/IMPERIAL

225 g/8 oz plain flour
pinch of salt
pinch of cayenne pepper
50 g/2 oz lard
50 g/2 oz margarine

100 g/4 oz Cheddar cheese
1 egg, beaten
little milk

1 Sift the flour, salt and pepper into a bowl and rub in the lard and margarine. Finely grate the cheese, stir into the flour mixture and add the egg and sufficient milk to make a firm dough. Turn on to a floured surface and knead lightly until smooth.
2 Roll out the pastry thinly and use to line 18 greased bun tins or 2 20-cm/8-inch foil flan cases. Prick well and bake the tartlet cases in a moderately hot oven (200°C, 400°F, Gas Mark 7) for about 15–20 minutes, until crisp and pale golden brown. Cool on a wire tray. Fill the flan cases with foil and baking beans and bake blind in a moderately hot oven as above for 20–25 minutes.
3 Freeze in rigid-based containers for protection.
4 Unpack and place on a baking sheet. Reheat from frozen in a moderately hot oven as above for 10 minutes. Spoon in chosen filling and serve.

**Prawn tartlet filling:** Mix 100 g/4 oz shelled prawns with 4 tablespoons thick mayonnaise and 2 chopped hard-boiled eggs. Garnish each tartlet with a tiny sprig of parsley.

**Mushroom tartlet filling:** Sauté 100 g/4 oz sliced button mushrooms in very little butter until golden. Cool and mix with 4 tablespoons thick mayonnaise and 2 tablespoons well-drained and finely chopped canned red pimento.

## Polish pasties

### Makes 8 pasties

METRIC/IMPERIAL

100 g/4 oz potato
350 g/12 oz boneless rabbit
100 g/4 oz shredded red cabbage
1 teaspoon dried basil

1 medium onion, chopped
few drops of Tabasco
salt and pepper
3 tablespoons beef stock
450 g/1 lb shortcrust pastry (see page 67)

when serving:
1 egg, beaten

1 Finely dice potato and rabbit and mix with the red cabbage, basil, onion and Tabasco. Season to taste and moisten with the stock.
2 Roll out the pastry and use to cut 8 20-cm/8-inch circles.
3 Divide the filling between the circles, fold each one over to form a semi circle, dampen the edges, seal well and flute.
4 Freeze before cooking.
5 Arrange the pasties on a greased baking sheet and brush with beaten egg. Bake from frozen in a hot oven (220°C, 425°F, Gas Mark 7) for 15 minutes. Reduce heat to moderate (180°C, 350°F, Gas Mark 4) and bake for a further 35 minutes.

## Sausage wraps

Roll out 225 g/8 oz cheese pastry (see page 68) and cut into 8 strips, each 2·5 cm/1 inch wide and about 25 cm/10 inches long. Brush the strips with beaten egg and wind each one round a large pork or beef sausage, to almost enclose it completely. Press the edges together to seal and tuck the ends underneath. Place the wrapped sausages on a greased baking sheet and bake in a moderately hot oven (200°C, 400°F, Gas Mark 6) for about 25 minutes, until the pastry is golden brown. Freeze in polythene containers and when required, place the sausage wraps on a baking sheet and reheat from frozen in a moderately hot oven as above for 15–20 minutes.

## Cheese straws

Roll out 225 g/8 oz cheese pastry thinly and cut into large rectangles. Place these on greased baking sheets and cut into thin strips, separating them slightly as you cut. Sprinkle lightly with 50 g/2 oz finely grated cheese and bake in a moderately hot oven (200°C, 400°F, Gas Mark 6) for 10–15 minutes, until pale golden. Freeze in polythene containers. When required, unpack and defrost at room temperature.

## Almond and cherry flan

**Makes 4–6 portions**

METRIC/IMPERIAL
| | |
|---|---|
| 175 g/6 oz shortcrust pastry (see page 67) | 40 g/1½ oz flour |
| 50 g/2 oz butter | 50 g/2 oz ground almonds |
| 50 g/2 oz castor sugar | 50 g/2 oz digestive biscuits, crushed |
| 1 egg, beaten | 0·75 kg/1½ lb cherries, stoned |
| ½ teaspoon almond essence | |

*when serving:*
sifted icing sugar

1 Roll out the pastry and use to line a 20-cm/8-inch foil flan case. Bake 'blind' in a moderately hot oven (190°C, 375°F, Gas Mark 5) for 15 minutes.
2 Cream the butter and sugar together and gradually beat in the egg and almond essence. Fold in the flour and ground almonds.
3 Sprinkle the biscuit crumbs in the pastry case, cover with the cherries and spread the almond mixture over the top.
4 Bake in the oven for about 35 minutes until golden brown on top. Cool.
5 Freeze in the foil case.
6 Reheat from frozen in a moderately hot oven as above for about 30 minutes and sift the top with icing sugar before serving.

## Nutty pear dumplings

METRIC/IMPERIAL
| | |
|---|---|
| 4 large ripe pears | 450 g/1 lb shortcrust pastry (see page 67) |
| 2 tablespoons brown sugar | egg, beaten |
| 25 g/1 oz chopped mixed nuts | |

1 Peel and core the pears. Mix together the sugar and nuts and use to stuff the centres of the pears.
2 Divide the pastry into 4 pieces and roll out each one until large enough to enclose a pear. Wrap the pastry round the pears, dampen the edges and seal well together.
3 Place the dumplings on a greased baking sheet, brush with the beaten egg and cook in a moderate oven (180°C, 350°F, Gas Mark 4) for about 40 minutes, until golden brown.
4 Wrap individually in foil for freezing.
5 Reheat from frozen still sealed in foil packs in a hot oven (220°C, 425°F, Gas Mark 7) for about 20 minutes. Open up the foil and return to the oven for a further 10 minutes.

### Variations:
**Italian dumplings:** Substitute peaches for the pears and ¼ teaspoon ground cinnamon instead of the nuts.

**Apple dumplings:** Substitute dessert apples for the pears and fill the centres with ground almonds mixed with stale cake crumbs.

**Apricot peanut butter dumplings:** Substitute apricots for the pears and stuff with 4 tablespoons peanut butter before sealing in the pastry cases.

## Frangipan orange tartlets

**Makes 24 tartlets**

METRIC/IMPERIAL
| | |
|---|---|
| 225 g/8 oz shortcrust pastry (see page 67) | finely grated rind and juice of ½ orange |
| 100 g/4 oz butter | 50 g/2 oz icing sugar, sifted |
| 100 g/4 oz castor sugar | ¼ teaspoon oil |
| 2 eggs, beaten | |
| 100 g/4 oz ground almonds | |

1 Roll out the pastry thinly, cut out 24 6·5-cm/2½-inch circles with a biscuit cutter and use to line bun tins.
2 Cream the butter and castor sugar together and gradually beat in the eggs.
3 Stir in the ground almonds, orange rind and juice.
4 Use this mixture to fill the pastry cases and bake in a moderately hot oven (190°C, 375°F, Gas Mark 5) for 20 minutes or until the filling is well-risen and golden brown. Cool on a wire tray.
5 Mix the icing sugar with the oil and sufficient orange juice to give a coating consistency. Ice the tops of the tartlets and allow decoration to set before freezing.

# Sweet rum custard tart

**Makes 6 portions**

METRIC/IMPERIAL
100 g/4 oz shortcrust
 pastry (see page 67)

50 g/2 oz castor sugar
300 ml/½ pint milk

filling:
2 eggs
25 g/1 oz flour
75 ml/3 fl oz rum

when serving:
150 ml/¼ pint whipping
 cream
little grated chocolate

1 Roll out the pastry and use to line a 17·5-cm/7-inch foil flan case.
2 Beat together all the ingredients for the filling or liquidise in a blender.
3 Pour the filling into the pastry case and bake in a moderately hot oven (200°C, 400°F, Gas Mark 6) for 25 minutes, or until the custard is set.
4 Open freeze before covering.
5 Uncover and defrost at room temperature for about 4 hours. Cover with whipped cream and decorate with grated chocolate.

# Lemon curd bakewell tart

**Makes 6 portions**

METRIC/IMPERIAL
100 g/4 oz shortcrust
 pastry (see page 67)
50 g/2 oz lemon curd
100 g/4 oz butter
100 g/4 oz castor sugar

2 eggs, beaten
75 g/3 oz self-raising flour
50 g/2 oz ground
 almonds

when serving:
little sifted icing sugar

1 Roll out the pastry and use to line a 17·5-cm/7-inch deep flan tin or deep foil flan case. Spread the base with the lemon curd.
2 Cream together the butter and sugar. Gradually beat in the egg. Sift the flour and fold into the creamed mixture with the ground almonds.
3 Spread over the lemon curd and bake in a moderately hot oven (200°C, 400°F, Gas Mark 6) for 30 minutes.
4 Open freeze before removing from the tin if used.
5 Defrost for 4 hours at room temperature and sprinkle with icing sugar before serving.

**Variations:**
**Fruity bakewell:** Substitute 40 g/1½ oz grated dessert apple for the ground almonds and add 25 g/1 oz sultanas at the same time.

**Almond and cherry bakewell:** Spread 50 g/2 oz chopped glacé cherries over the pastry instead of the jam and add ½ teaspoon almond essence to the filling.

# Mincemeat and banana pies

**Makes 18 pies**

METRIC/IMPERIAL
350 g/12 oz butter
450 g/1 lb plain flour
2 teaspoons castor sugar
2 egg yolks

4 tablespoons iced water
1 large ripe banana
450 g/1 lb mincemeat
little milk

when serving:
castor sugar

1 Rub the butter into the flour and sugar. Add the egg yolks and half the water and gradually mix these into the dry ingredients, adding the remaining water a little at a time. Wrap the dough and chill for 1 hour.
2 Roll out the pastry and cut out about 18 large and 18 small rounds with a fluted biscuit cutter. Place the larger rounds in greased bun tins.
3 Mash the banana and combine with the mincemeat. Divide between the pastry cases. Cover with the smaller pastry rounds, dampen the edges and seal well together.
4 Brush the pies with milk and bake in a hot oven (220°C, 425°F, Gas Mark 7) for 5 minutes. Reduce heat to moderately hot (220°C, 400°F, Gas Mark 6) and bake for a further 10 minutes, until golden brown.
5 Freeze in a rigid-based container for protection.
6 Arrange the frozen pies on a baking sheet and reheat from frozen in a moderately hot oven as above for about 15 minutes. Sprinkle with sugar before serving.

# Coconut congress tarts

**Makes 24 tarts**

METRIC/IMPERIAL
350 g/12 oz shortcrust
 pastry (see page 67)
4 tablespoons red jam
100 g/4 oz butter
100 g/4 oz castor sugar
2 eggs, beaten

½ teaspoon vanilla
 essence
50 g/2 oz self-raising flour
50 g/2 oz desiccated
 coconut

1 Roll out the pastry and cut rounds with a fluted biscuit cutter to line 24 greased bun tins.
2 Cream the butter and sugar until light and fluffy and gradually beat in the egg and vanilla essence. Fold in the flour and coconut.
3 Place a little jam in the base of each tart and top with the coconut filling.
4 Bake in a moderate oven (180°C, 350°F, Gas Mark 4) for about 30 minutes.
5 Freeze in a rigid-based container for protection.
6 Unpack and arrange on a serving dish to defrost.

**Variations:**
**Orange congress tarts:** Substitute 50 g/2 oz ground almonds for the coconut, add the finely grated zest of 1 orange to the filling mixture and use marmalade instead of the red jam.

**Chocolate congress tarts:** Substitute 25 g/1 oz ground almonds and 2 tablespoons cocoa for the coconut and use chocolate spread instead of the red jam.

# Spiced plum squares

## Makes 12 squares, 12 portions

METRIC/IMPERIAL

| | |
|---|---|
| 0·75 kg/1½ lb shortcrust pastry (see page 67) | 150 g/5 oz sugar |
| 1 kg/2 lb plums | 2 teaspoons ground cinnamon |
| finely grated rind and juice of 1 lemon | 1 egg white |

1 Roll out just over half the pastry and use to line a large square roasting tin or ovenproof dish about 30 cm/12 inches by 22·5 cm/9 inches.
2 Halve and stone the plums and mix with the lemon rind and juice, 100 g/4 oz of the sugar and half the cinnamon. Spread this mixture in the pastry case.
3 Roll out the remaining pastry to make a lid, dampen the edges and seal well together. Prick the top with a fork. Whisk the egg white lightly and use to brush the pastry. Mix together the remaining sugar and cinnamon and sprinkle over the top.
4 Bake in a moderate oven (180°C, 350°F, Gas Mark 4) for about 45 minutes.
5 Freeze in the baking tin.
6 Uncover and reheat from frozen in a hot oven (220°C, 425°F, Gas Mark 7) for 25 minutes. Cut into squares before serving.

### Variation:

**Spiced apples squares:** Substitute 1 kg/2 lb cooking apples for the plums. Peel and coarsely grate them before mixing with the lemon rind, spice and sugar.

# Open apricot tart

## Makes 1 tart, 4–6 portions

METRIC/IMPERIAL

| | |
|---|---|
| 175 g/6 oz shortcrust pastry (see page 67) | 1 teaspoon lemon juice |
| 3 tablespoons apricot jam | 2 teaspoons ground mace |
| 350 g/12 oz apricots, halved | 1 tablespoon flour |
| | 2 tablespoons castor sugar |

1 Roll out the pastry and use to line a 20-cm/8-inch foil flan case. Spread the base with the apricot jam.
2 Remove the stones from the apricots and arrange them cut side down on the pastry base. Sprinkle with the lemon juice. Mix together the spice, flour and castor sugar and sprinkle over the fruit.
3 Bake in a moderately hot oven (200°C, 400°F, Gas Mark 6) for about 40 minutes.
4 Freeze in the container.
5 Reheat from frozen in a moderately hot oven as above for about 30 minutes.

### Variations:

**Open pineapple tart:** Substitute a 425-g/15-oz can of pineapple pieces for the apricots. Drain well on absorbent kitchen paper before arranging in the pastry case.

**Open plum tart:** Substitute 350 g/12 oz ripe plums for the apricots and use plum jam instead of apricot jam.

**Open greengage tart:** Substitute 350 g/12 oz ripe greengages for the apricots and use greengage jam instead of apricot jam.

**Open cherry tart:** Substitute 450 g/1 lb cherries for the apricots. Stone them before arranging in the pastry case and use any red jam instead of the apricot jam.

# Double crust rhubarb tarts

## Makes 2 tarts, 8–12 portions

METRIC/IMPERIAL

| | |
|---|---|
| 0·5 kg/1¼ lb shortcrust pastry (see page 67) | 2 teaspoons cornflour |
| 1 egg white | 75 g/3 oz castor sugar |
| 1 kg/2 lb rhubarb | rind of 1 orange, grated |

1 Roll out two-thirds of the pastry and use to line two greased 20-cm/8-inch foil plates. Brush with egg white.
2 Cut the rhubarb into short lengths and divide between the pastry cases. Mix together the cornflour, castor sugar and orange zest and sprinkle over the rhubarb.
3 Roll out the remaining pastry and use to cut two lids. Dampen the edges and seal well together. Decorate with pastry trimmings and brush all over with remaining egg white.
4 Freeze before cooking.
5 Uncover and cut a steam vent. Bake from frozen in a hot oven (220°C, 425°F, Gas Mark 7) for about 30 minutes. Sprinkle with sugar before serving if wished.

### Variations:

**Rhubarb and ginger tarts:** Substitute ¾ teaspoon ground ginger for the orange zest and add 1 tablespoon chopped preserved ginger to the rhubarb.

**Apple and rhubarb tarts:** Use 450 g/1 lb prepared cooking apple slices and 450 g/1 lb rhubarb for the filling and lemon rind instead of orange rind.

**Strawberry and rhubarb tarts:** Use 450 g/1 lb firm strawberries and 450 g/1 lb rhubarb for the filling. Reduce the sugar to 50 g/2 oz.

**Pear sultana and rhubarb tarts:** Peel, core and slice 450 g/1 lb firm dessert pears and use with 225 g/8 oz rhubarb and 50 g/2 oz sultanas as the filling. Reduce the sugar to 50 g/2 oz.

**Cherry apple and cinnamon tarts:** Stone 450 g/1 lb ripe cherries and use with 225 g/8 oz prepared cooking apple slices for the filling. Use 1 teaspoon ground cinnamon instead of the orange rind. Reduce the sugar to 50 g/2 oz if the cherries are sweet.

# Flaky pastry

## Forfar Bridies

**Makes 4 Bridies, 4 portions**

METRIC/IMPERIAL

| | |
|---|---|
| 450 g/1 lb flaky pastry mix | 50 g/2 oz shredded suet |
| 6–8 tablespoons cold water | 1 small onion, grated |
| 450 g/1 lb topside, rump or chuck steak | salt and pepper |
| | 1 egg, beaten |

1 Make up the pastry mix with the water as per the instructions on the packet. Roll out the pastry thinly and cut into four 25-cm/10-inch squares.
2 Cut the meat into very thin strips and mix with the suet, onion and seasoning to taste.
3 Divide the filling between the pastry squares, dampen the edges, fold over the pastry and seal the edges well together to make triangular Bridies.
4 Arrange on a greased baking sheet and make a small hole in the top of each Bridie to allow the steam to escape. Brush with beaten egg and bake in a moderately hot oven (190°C, 375°F, Gas Mark 5) for 30–40 minutes, until well risen and golden brown.
5 Pack in layers with dividers for freezing.
6 Reheat from frozen in a moderately hot oven (200°C, 400°F, Gas Mark 6) for about 30 minutes.

## Apple and ginger turnovers

**Makes 12 turnovers, 12 portions**

METRIC/IMPERIAL

| | |
|---|---|
| 450 g/1 lb flaky pastry mix | 4 pieces preserved ginger, chopped |
| 6–8 tablespoons cold water | 50 g/2 oz sugar |
| 450 g/1 lb cooking apples, peeled | ½ teaspoon ground ginger |
| | little milk |

1 Make up the pastry mix with the water as per the instructions on the packet. Divide the pastry in half, roll out each piece to a rectangle about 37·5 cm/15 inches by 25 cm/10 inches and cut into six 12·5-cm/5-inch squares.
2 Core and slice the apples and mix with the chopped ginger. Combine the sugar and spice and add to the apple mixture. Divide between the pastry squares. Dampen the edges and seal well together. Chill for 30 minutes.
3 Brush with milk and bake in a hot oven (220°C, 425°F, Gas Mark 7) for about 20 minutes.
4 Freeze in a rigid-based container for protection.
5 Unpack and arrange on a baking sheet then reheat from frozen in a hot oven as above for about 15 minutes.

## Cherry and almond pasties

**Makes 8 pasties (8 portions)**

METRIC/IMPERIAL

| | |
|---|---|
| 450-g/1-lb packet flaky pastry mix | 100 g/4 oz granulated sugar |
| 6–8 tablespoons cold water | 50 g/2 oz ground almonds |
| 450 g/1 lb black cherries, stoned | little milk |

1 Make up the pastry mix with the water and roll and fold it as per the instructions on the pack. Chill while you prepare the filling.
2 Stone the cherries and mix them lightly with the sugar and almonds.
3 Roll out the pastry and divide into 8 12·5-cm/5-inch squares. Divide the cherry filling among the squares, fold over the pastry, dampen the edges and seal well together, to make triangular pasties.
4 Pierce a small hole in the top of each one, then arrange on a greased baking sheet and brush with milk.
5 Bake in a moderately hot oven (200°C, 400°F, Gas Mark 6) for about 15 minutes, until golden brown.
6 Pack carefully in layers with dividers before freezing.
7 Defrost at room temperature and serve cold, or reheat from frozen on a baking sheet in a moderately hot oven as above for about 20 minutes.

**Variation:**

Apricot and apple pasties: Substitute 225 g/8 oz stoned and quartered apricots and 225 g/8 oz prepared cooking apple slices for the cherries.

# Puff pastry

## Creamy veal and bacon pie

### Makes 6 portions

METRIC/IMPERIAL

| | |
|---|---|
| 4 rashers streaky bacon, derinded | ½ teaspoon sugar |
| 0·75 kg/1½ lb pie veal, cubed | 2 teaspoons lemon juice |
| | 225 g/8 oz frozen puff pastry, defrosted |
| 1 medium onion, chopped | 1 egg, beaten |
| 300 ml/½ pint water | 150 ml/¼ pint double cream |
| salt and pepper | |
| 1 teaspoon chopped parsley | |

1 Dice the bacon and place in a saucepan with the veal, onion, water and seasoning to taste. Bring to the boil, cover and simmer for about 55 minutes, until the veal is tender. Stir in the sugar, parsley and lemon juice and pour into a 1·5-litre/2½-pint pie dish. Cool.
2 Roll out the pastry to form a lid, dampen the edges, seal well to the dish and flute. Decorate with pastry trimmings, make a hole in the top and brush all over with beaten egg.
3 Bake in a moderately hot oven (200°C, 400°F, Gas Mark 6) for 20 minutes. Pour the cream through the hole in the pastry using a funnel then shake the pie carefully to mix the juices. Return to the oven for a further 10 minutes.
4 Open freeze before packing.
5 Defrost and then reheat in a moderately hot oven (190°C, 375°F, Gas Mark 5) for about 40 minutes. Cover pastry with foil if necessary to prevent over-browning.

### Variation:

**Fruity veal and bacon pie:** Reduce the quantity of veal to 550 g/1¼ lb and omit the sugar. When the veal is tender add 100 g/4 oz drained chopped canned pineapple. Blend 1 tablespoon cornflour with 6 tablespoons pineapple syrup from the can and add to the pie in place of the cream.

## Party vol-au-vent cases

### Makes about 18 vol-au-vent cases.

METRIC/IMPERIAL

| | |
|---|---|
| 450 g/1 lb frozen puff pastry, defrosted | 1 egg, beaten |
| | 1 tablespoon water |

1 Roll out the pastry thinly and cut into 6·5-cm/2½-inch rounds with a fluted biscuit cutter. Beat the egg with the water and use to brush the pastry rounds. Place on damped baking sheets and cut halfway through the centre of each round with a 2·5-cm/1-inch cutter. Chill for 10 minutes. Bake in a hot oven (220°C, 425°F, Gas Mark 7) for about 10 minutes, until well risen, golden brown and crisp. Cool on a wire tray.
2 Remove the tops of the vol-au-vent cases and press down the soft pastry inside with the handle of a teaspoon.

3 Fill the vol-au-vents with the chosen filling, replace the pastry cap and freeze in layers with dividers.
4 Unpack filled vol-au-vents and defrost at room temperature for 3 hours. If required hot, reheat after defrosting in a moderately hot oven (190°C, 375°F, Gas Mark 5) for about 15 minutes.

### Variations:

**Curried turkey vol-au-vent filling:** Beat 1 teaspoon instant concentrated curry sauce or curry paste into 300 ml/½ pint Savoury white sauce (see page 60) with 100 g/4 oz chopped cooked turkey and 2 tablespoons finely chopped seedless raisins.

**Sweetbread vol-au-vent filling:** Stir 2 teaspoons lemon juice into 300 ml/½ pint Savoury white sauce (see page 60) with 100 g/4 oz chopped cooked sweetbreads and 50 g/2 oz chopped ham.

## Oxfordshire deep dish pie

### Makes 4–6 portions

METRIC/IMPERIAL

| | |
|---|---|
| 15 g/½ oz butter | 50 g/2 oz chopped candied peel |
| 0·75 kg/1½ lb prepared cooking apple slices | ½ teaspoon ground mixed spice |
| 2 teaspoons lemon juice | |
| 100 g/4 oz soft brown sugar | 225 g/8 oz frozen puff pastry, defrosted |
| 50 g/2 oz currants | little milk |

1 Grease a 1·5-litre/2½-pint pie dish with the butter.
2 Mix together the apple, lemon juice, sugar, currants, peel and spice and place in the pie dish.
3 Roll out the pastry and use to cover the fruit. Seal the edges and use pastry trimmings to decorate the top. Brush with milk.
4 Open freeze before cooking.
5 Uncover and cook from frozen in a hot oven (220°C, 425°F, Gas Mark 7) for 20 minutes then reduce heat to moderate (180°C, 350°F, Gas Mark 4) for about a further 15 minutes.

### Variations:

**Pear and plum pie:** Substitute 450 g/1 lb prepared firm dessert pear slices and 225 g/8 oz stoned and quartered plums for the apple slices.

**Greengage and almond pie:** Substitute halved and stoned greengages for the apple slices and use 50 g/2 oz ground almonds, 25 g/1 oz dry white breadcrumbs and ½ teaspoon almond essence instead of the currants, peel and spice.

**Blackberry and apple pie:** Use 450 g/1 lb prepared apple slices and 225 g/8 oz ripe blackberries.

## Chicken and corn pie

**Makes 6 portions**

METRIC/IMPERIAL

| | |
|---|---|
| 25 g/1 oz butter | few drops Tabasco pepper |
| 25 g/1 oz flour | sauce |
| 300 ml/½ pint milk | salt and pepper |
| 283-g/10-oz can | 225 g/8 oz puff pastry |
| cream-style corn | 1 egg, beaten |
| 0·5 kg/1¼ lb cooked | |
| chicken, diced | |

1 Place the butter, flour and milk in a saucepan and whisk over moderate heat until smooth and thick. Simmer for 2 minutes.
2 Remove from the heat, stir in the corn, cooked chicken and Tabasco. Season to taste with salt and pepper. Cool.
3 Place the chicken mixture in a foil pie dish.
4 Roll out the pastry and use to cover the pie. Dampen the edges and seal well to the container. Decorate with pastry trimmings. Brush with beaten egg.
5 Open freeze before packing.
6 Uncover and bake from frozen in a moderately hot oven (200°C, 400°F, Gas Mark 6) for about 45 minutes.

## Blackberry and apple puffs

**Makes 6 portions**

METRIC/IMPERIAL

| | |
|---|---|
| 450 g/1 lb puff pastry | 75 g/3 oz castor sugar |
| 1 large cooking apple | 1 egg, beaten |
| 225 g/8 oz blackberries | |

1 Roll out the pastry thinly and cut into six 15-cm/6-inch squares.
2 Peel, core and chop the apple, mix with the blackberries and sugar. Divide the filling among the pastry squares.
3 Brush the edges with beaten egg, fold over the pastry diagonally and seal the edges well. Decorate the border with the prongs of a fork. Brush all over with beaten egg.
4 Open freeze, then pack together in one container.
5 Unpack, place on a damped baking sheet and bake from frozen in a hot oven (220°C, 425°F, Gas Mark 7) for about 30 minutes, until well risen and golden brown.

# Choux pastry

## Basic choux puffs

**Makes about 32 puffs**

METRIC/IMPERIAL

| | |
|---|---|
| 150 g/5 oz plain flour | 300 ml/½ pint water |
| ¼ teaspoon salt | 4 eggs, beaten |
| 100 g/4 oz butter | |

1 Sift the flour and salt together. Place the butter and water in a saucepan and heat gently. When the butter has melted, bring the mixture to the boil. Remove from the heat immediately and add the flour all at once. Beat with a wooden spoon until the mixture is smooth and forms a ball which leaves the sides of the pan clean. Cool slightly then add the eggs, one at a time, beating well after each addition. The mixture should be smooth and glossy. Cool.
2 Place in a piping bag fitted with a 1-cm/½-inch nozzle. Pipe about 32 balls of paste, well apart, on greased baking sheets. Bake in a moderately hot oven (200°C, 400°F, Gas Mark 6) for about 25 minutes, until well risen, pale golden brown and crisp. Cool on a wire rack.
3 Pack in polythene bags.
4 Unpack and arrange the puffs on a baking sheet. Reheat and crisp from frozen in a moderately hot oven (190°C, 375°F, Gas Mark 5) for 7–8 minutes.

## Fillings for choux puffs

Although whipped cream is delicious inside these miniature cream buns, there are many other fillings which can be used instead. It is quite practical to freeze the puffs already filled with whipped cream or with some other filling, but this prevents you from crisping them up at serving time. My preferred method is to prepare the filling either just before or while the puffs are defrosting and crisping in the oven. The crisp cool puffs should be pierced at one side with the rounded handle of a small teaspoon. The filling can usually be inserted with the bowl of the spoon or can be forced in from a piping bag fitted with a small nozzle.

### Sweet fillings for choux puffs
The quantities given are sufficient to fill about 16 puffs and then to serve 4 people.

**Honey cream puffs:** Whisk a small can of evaporated milk until thick and add 2 tablespoons lemon juice, 1 teaspoon grated lemon rind and 1 tablespoon clear honey. Continue whisking for a further 2 minutes. Dissolve 1 tablespoon gelatine in 2 tablespoons water in a basin over hot water. Allow to cool. Whisk into the milk. When the mixture begins to set, use to fill the puffs. Serve the puffs, sprinkled with sifted icing sugar.

**Butterscotch ice cream buns:** Slice the tops off the puffs and press down the soft centre with the back of a teaspoon and fill each with a small scoop of vanilla ice cream. Replace the tops and serve with Smooth butterscotch sauce (see page 60).

**Minty chocolate ice cream buns:** Make these as above but substitute mint and chocolate ice cream for the vanilla ice cream and serve with Chocolate sauce (see page 59).

## Savoury choux puffs

Add 50 g/2 oz finely grated hard cheese, $\frac{1}{2}$ teaspoon salt and $\frac{1}{4}$ teaspoon pepper to the choux paste after adding the flour. Bake and freeze as for Basic choux puffs.

### Fillings for savoury choux puffs

**Cheese filling:** Finely dice 50 g/2 oz Gouda cheese and stir into 150 ml/$\frac{1}{4}$ pint cold cheese sauce (see page 60). Use to fill the puffs as for Butterscotch ice cream buns.

**Tuna filling:** Beat 2 tablespoons mayonnaise into 150 ml/$\frac{1}{4}$ pint Savoury white sauce (see page 60). Fold in 75 g/3 oz drained and flaked tuna and adjust the seasoning if necessary. Fill the puffs as above.

**Chicken filling:** Beat 2 tablespoons mayonnaise into 150 ml/$\frac{1}{4}$ pint Savoury white sauce (see page 60). Fold in 75 g/3 oz chopped cooked chicken and adjust the seasoning if necessary. Fill the puffs as above.

## Bacon and tomato gougère

### Makes 2 gougères, 8 portions

METRIC/IMPERIAL

| | |
|---|---|
| 225 g/8 oz streaky bacon, derinded | 300 ml/$\frac{1}{2}$ pint chicken stock |
| 25 g/1 oz butter | salt and pepper |
| 2 medium onions, chopped | 1 quantity savoury choux paste /(see above) |
| 225 g/8 oz tomatoes, peeled | 100 g/4 oz Lancashire cheese, crumbled |
| 25 g/1 oz flour | |

1 Chop the bacon, melt the butter and use to fry the onion and bacon gently until the onion is soft. Chop the tomatoes and add to the pan with the flour. Stir well and cook for 2 minutes. Gradually add the stock and bring to the boil, stirring constantly. Season to taste and cool.
2 Make the choux paste and spoon round the edges of two medium-sized greased foil containers. Divide the filling between the two centres and sprinkle with the crumbled cheese.
3 Freeze before cooking.
4 Uncover and bake from frozen in a moderately hot oven (200°C, 400°F, Gas Mark 6) for 45–50 minutes, or until well risen and golden brown.

# Suet pastry

## Minced beef and kidney puddings

### Makes 2 puddings, 8 portions

METRIC/IMPERIAL

| | |
|---|---|
| 450 g/1 lb self-raising flour | pinch of pepper |
| 225 g/8 oz shredded suet | water to mix |
| pinch of salt | |

*filling:*

| | |
|---|---|
| 225 g/8 oz ox kidney | about 300 ml/$\frac{1}{2}$ pint beef stock |
| 2 tablespoons seasoned flour | salt and pepper |
| 0·75 kg/1$\frac{1}{2}$ lb minced beef | |
| 2 medium onions, chopped | |

1 Combine the flour, suet, salt and pepper and add sufficient water to make a firm dough. Roll out two-thirds of the pastry and use to line two 1-litre/1$\frac{3}{4}$-pint foil pudding basins.
2 Trim the kidney and cut into small pieces. Coat with seasoned flour. Place the minced beef, kidney and onion in layers in the two pudding cases, sprinkling in any remaining seasoned flour. Add beef stock to come three-quarters of the way up the puddings and season to taste.
3 Roll out the remaining pastry and use to make two lids. Moisten the edges and seal well to the puddings. Cover the basins with foil and steam or boil for 3–4 hours. Cool.
4 Cover with fresh foil before freezing.
5 Reheat from frozen by boiling or steaming for about 1 hour.

### Variation:

**Pork and tomato puddings:** Substitute 0·75 kg/1$\frac{1}{2}$ lb diced bladebone of pork for the minced beef and kidney and add 1 teaspoon dried sage, 1 teaspoon Worcestershire sauce and a 390-g/14-oz can of tomatoes instead of the stock. Season well.

## Baked fruit and jam roly-poly

### Makes 6–8 portions

METRIC/IMPERIAL

| | |
|---|---|
| 225 g/8 oz plain flour | cold water |
| $\frac{1}{2}$ teaspoon salt | 3 tablespoons apricot jam |
| 2 teaspoons baking powder | 100 g/4 oz prepared diced cooking apple |
| 100 g/4 oz shredded suet | 50 g/2 oz sultanas |

1 Sift the flour with the salt and baking powder. Stir in the suet and add sufficient cold water to make a stiff dough. Roll out on a floured surface to a rectangle about 25 cm/10 inches by 20 cm/8 inches.
2 Spread the jam over the pastry to within 2·5 cm/1 inch of the edges and scatter the apple and sultanas on top. Dampen the edges and roll up loosely. Seal the ends and tuck them underneath.

3 Place on a foil-lined baking sheet with the seal underneath, slash the top and bake in a moderately hot oven (190°C, 375°F, Gas Mark 5) for about 40 minutes.

4 Wrap the roly-poly in the foil on which it was baked.

5 Place on a baking sheet, open up the foil and reheat from frozen in a moderately hot oven as above for about 35 minutes.

### Variations:

**Strawberry and sultana roly-poly:** Substitute 175 g/6 oz strawberry pie filling for the apricot jam and cooking apple. Stir in the sultanas and add 25 g/1 oz chopped almonds before spreading on the pastry.

**Steamed raisin roll:** Make the suet pastry and roll out as above. Substitute 3 tablespoons golden syrup for the apricot jam and scatter over 100 g/4 oz seedless raisins and 50 g/2 oz fresh white breadcrumbs instead of the apple and sultanas. Roll up, wrap loosely in foil and steam for about 2 hours. Overwrap before freezing. To reheat, remove the overwrap and steam from frozen in the original foil covering for 1¼ hours.

# Layered orange and apple pudding

## Makes 2 puddings, 8 portions

METRIC/IMPERIAL

| | |
|---|---|
| 450 g/1 lb self-raising flour | 225 g/8 oz shredded suet water to mix |

filling:

| | |
|---|---|
| 2 large cooking apples | 2 tablespoons chunky marmalade |
| 1 large orange | |
| 25 g/1 oz butter | |
| 2 tablespoons soft brown sugar | |

1 Combine the flour and suet, and add sufficient water to make a firm dough. Roll out two-thirds of the pastry and use to line two 1-litre/1¾-pint foil pudding basins.

2 Peel, core and roughly chop the apples. Grate the rind from the orange, peel it and divide into segments.

3 Melt the butter, stir in the sugar and marmalade. Add the apple and stir until coated.

4 Fill the basins with layers of the apple mixture and orange segments.

5 Roll out the remaining pastry and use to make two lids. Moisten the edges and seal well to the puddings. Cover the basins with foil and steam or boil for 3 hours. Cool.

6 Cover with fresh foil before freezing.

7 Reheat by boiling or steaming from frozen for about 1 hour.

# Freezable sweet treats

Here we come to some of the most delicate items you are likely to store in the freezer. Biscuits and cookies rarely cause trouble because they do store very well, layered in rigid-based containers. Nevertheless, I have given recipes for those who prefer to store the dough in a roll and cut off slices to be baked at serving time. If you bake too many, those left over can still be stored by any conventional method, even in the biscuit tin.

## Family favourite puddings

No freezer stock for the average family would be complete without a few puddings. There is no need to consign your pudding basins or pie dishes to a long stay in the freezer if you use shaped foil containers. With careful treatment these can usually be used a second time. If steamed puddings are a 'must' with your family, it is worth while making up quite a large quantity of the basic sponge mixture and filling several pudding basins. Steam one for today and freeze the others uncooked. You can then steam the other puddings, one at a time, when you need them. Crumbled and baked sponge puddings are no trouble to the cook if the same method of preparation is followed, and it is an advantage that all these can start cooking from the frozen state and do not have to be defrosted first.

## Cakes for all occasions

The demand for small cakes, larger ones of the cut-and-come-again variety, and cheesecakes, never seems to stop. All cakes, especially decorated ones, should be open frozen before packing closely. Unless very delicate, large cakes slide easily into a bag if placed first on a firm base.

Most damage occurs when rummaging in the freezer for a lost item, or during unpacking when cakes are partially defrosted. Do remove wrapping while cakes are still fully frozen and hard. Since small fancy cakes are some trouble to make, they deserve more care than jumbling together in a bag. Square or oblong rigid-based containers give the best protection and if cakes are carefully piped you may wish to search out some containers that are shallow enough to allow the cakes to be packed in a single layer.

## Delicate cold sweets

All sorts of mousses and trifles find their way into the average freezer. Individual servings ensure that there is no damage between freezer and table. Nor should there be any damage to a mousse frozen in a large serving dish if one avoids the rather ambitious frozen soufflé which requires to be protected above the rim of the soufflé dish. Trifles made with canned custard seem to be the most successful and if decorations on any mousse or trifle are kept below the rim of the dish (which is then tightly covered with cling wrap or foil) the decoration is safe from harm. Commercial ice cream makes it uneconomic to prepare your own using eggs and cream except for very rare occasions, but I have included a basic ice cream recipe using evaporated milk which won't break the bank. There are many ways to dress up ice cream to produce an elaborate home-made dessert with ease. Time is vital when planning to remove frozen desserts from the freezer to the refrigerator so that the consistency is just right when you wish to serve them. On many recipes special instructions are given to ensure this.

# Hot puddings and cakes

## Lemon curd sponge pudding

### Makes 4 portions

METRIC/IMPERIAL

| | |
|---|---|
| 2 tablespoons lemon curd | pinch of salt |
| 100 g/4 oz butter | finely grated rind of I |
| 100 g/4 oz castor sugar | lemon |
| 2 eggs, beaten | I tablespoon lemon juice |
| 175 g/6 oz self-raising flour | |

1 Place the lemon curd in the base of a 1-litre/1¾-pint foil pudding basin.
2 Cream the butter and sugar together and gradually beat in the egg. Sift the flour and salt and fold into the creamed mixture with the lemon rind and juice. Spoon into the pudding basin.
3 Cover with foil and freeze before cooking.
4 Steam from frozen for about 2¼ hours and turn out on a serving dish.

### Variations:

**Marmalade sponge pudding:** Substitute 2 tablespoons orange jelly marmalade for the lemon curd and use orange rind and juice instead of lemon.

**Jam sponge pudding:** Substitute 2 tablespoons red jam for the lemon curd and use 1 tablespoon milk instead of the lemon juice.

**Grapefruit syrup sponge pudding:** Substitute 2 tablespoons golden syrup for the lemon curd and use 1 tablespoon grapefruit juice and the rind of ½ grapefruit instead of the lemon rind and juice.

## Apple and pineapple crumble

### Makes 4–6 portions

METRIC/IMPERIAL

| | |
|---|---|
| 75 g/3 oz drained canned pineapple pieces | 100 g/4 oz castor sugar |
| 350 g/12 oz prepared cooking apple slices | 75 g/3 oz butter |
| 25 g/1 oz mixed peel, chopped | 175 g/6 oz plain flour |

1 Chop the pineapple and mix with the apple and peel. Stir in 25 g/1 oz of the sugar and place in a deep foil container.
2 Rub the butter into the flour and stir in the remaining sugar. Sprinkle over the apple mixture.
3 Freeze before cooking.
4 Uncover and bake from frozen in a moderately hot oven (190°C, 375°F, Gas Mark 5) for about 50 minutes, until golden brown on top.

### Variations:

**Rhubarb and raspberry crumble:** Substitute 350 g/12 oz prepared rhubarb slices for the apple, 75 g/3 oz raspberries for the pineapple. Add extra sugar if necessary and omit the peel.

**Pear, sultana and apricot crumble:** Substitute 350 g/12 oz peeled, cored and sliced dessert pear for the apple, 75 g/3 oz drained canned apricot halves for the pineapple and 25 g/1 oz sultanas for the peel.

**Greengage and peach crumble:** Substitute 350 g/12 oz halved and stoned greengages for the apple and 1 large ripe peeled, stoned and sliced peach or 75 g/3 oz drained canned peach slices for the pineapple.

## Eve's plum pudding

### Makes 4–6 portions

METRIC/IMPERIAL

| | |
|---|---|
| 0·5 kg/1¼ lb plums | ¼ teaspoon vanilla |
| 150 g/5 oz castor sugar | essence |
| 75 g/3 oz butter | 100 g/4 oz self-raising flour |
| I egg, beaten | |

*when serving:*
castor sugar

1 Halve and stone the plums and place in a deep foil container with 50 g/2 oz of the sugar.
2 Cream the butter and sugar together and gradually beat in the egg and vanilla essence. Fold in the flour and spread this mixture over the plums.
3 Freeze before cooking.
4 Uncover and bake from frozen in a moderately hot oven (190°C, 375°F, Gas Mark 5) for about 50 minutes, until golden brown on top. Sprinkle with sugar before serving.

### Variations:

**Eve's blackberry and apple pudding:** Substitute 350 g/12 oz blackberries and 225 g/8 oz prepared cooking apple slices for the plums.

**Eve's apple and grape pudding:** Substitute 350 g/12 oz prepared cooking apple slices and 225 g/8 oz seedless, or halved and seeded grapes for the plums. Add a pinch of ground mixed spice to the sugar for sprinkling over the fruit.

**Eve's cherry pudding:** Substitute 450 g/1 lb stoned cherries for the plums and use almond essence instead of the vanilla.

## All-in-one ginger pudding

### Makes 6 portions

METRIC/IMPERIAL

| | |
|---|---|
| 175 g/6 oz soft margarine | 75 g/3 oz sultanas |
| 175 g/6 oz soft brown sugar | I piece preserved ginger, chopped |
| 3 eggs | I tablespoon ginger syrup from jar |
| 175 g/6 oz self-raising flour | 3 tablespoons golden syrup |
| 2 teaspoons baking powder | 2 tablespoons lemon juice |
| 1¼ teaspoons ground ginger | |

1 Place the first six ingredients in a bowl and beat for 2–3 minutes, until well blended. Stir in the sultanas and place in a large greased foil container.
2 Bake in a moderate oven (180°C, 350°F, Gas Mark 4) for about 50 minutes, until golden brown.
3 Meanwhile, place the remaining ingredients in a saucepan and heat gently, stirring. When the pudding is removed from the oven, spoon over the ginger mixture and allow to cool.
4 Freeze in the foil container and cover with foil.
5 Place still covered with foil in a moderately hot oven (190°C, 375°F, Gas Mark 5) for about 50 minutes.

### Variations:
**Chocolate and ginger pudding:** Substitute 25 g/1 oz cocoa for 25 g/1 oz of the flour.

**Spiced date pudding:** Substitute 1½ teaspoons mixed spice for the ground ginger, 75 g/3 oz chopped stoned dates for the sultanas and 1 extra tablespoon of golden syrup in place of the ginger syrup. Omit the chopped ginger.

## One-step Victoria sandwich

### Makes I cake, 6–8 portions

METRIC/IMPERIAL
| | |
|---|---|
| 100 g/4 oz soft margarine | I teaspoon baking powder |
| 100 g/4 oz castor sugar | 4 tablespoons red jam |
| ½ teaspoon vanilla essence | icing sugar |
| 2 eggs | |
| 100 g/4 oz self-raising flour | |

1 Place the first six ingredients in a mixing bowl and beat well for about 3 minutes, until smooth.
2 Grease two 17·5-cm/7-inch sandwich tins, line the bases with greaseproof paper and grease the paper. Divide the mixture between the tins and smooth the tops.
3 Bake in a moderate oven (160°C, 325°F, Gas Mark 3) for about 30 minutes, until golden brown and firm to the touch. Cool on a wire rack.
4 Sandwich the cake layers together with the jam and sift the top with icing sugar.
5 Open freeze before packing.
6 Uncover while still frozen and allow to defrost at room temperature.

### Variations:
**Citrus sandwich:** Substitute the finely grated rind of 1 orange or 1 large lemon for the vanilla essence. Sandwich together with lemon curd.

**Sweet coffee sandwich:** Dissolve 2 teaspoons instant coffee in 1 tablespoon boiling water. Cool and add to the cake mixture in place of the vanilla essence. Sandwich together with set honey.

**Chocolate almond sandwich:** Blend 2 tablespoons cocoa with 2 tablespoons boiling water. Cool and add to the cake mixture with 25 g/1 oz ground almonds. Omit the vanilla essence. Sandwich together with chocolate spread.

## Citrus ring cake

### Makes I cake, 6–8 portions

METRIC/IMPERIAL
| | |
|---|---|
| I quantity citrus flavour Victoria sandwich mixture (see this page ) | finely grated rind of ½ lemon |
| 75 g/3 oz butter | finely grated rind of ½ orange |
| 225 g/8 oz icing sugar, sifted | 2 tablespoons orange or lemon juice |

1 Make the cake mixture and turn into a greased and floured 22·5-cm/9-inch ring cake tin. Smooth the top.
2 Bake in a moderate oven (160°C, 325°F, Gas Mark 3) for about 40 minutes, until golden brown and firm to the touch. Turn out and cool on a wire rack.
3 Cream the butter with the icing sugar until smooth. Add the fruit rinds and gradually beat in the fruit juice.
4 Spread the icing over the ring cake to cover it completely and mark into swirls with the tip of a round-bladed knife.
5 Open freeze before packing.
6 Uncover while frozen and defrost at room temperature.

# Coffee fudge cake

## Makes I cake, 6–8 portions

METRIC/IMPERIAL

| | |
|---|---|
| I quantity coffee flavour Victoria sandwich mixture (see page 79) | I tablespoon coffee essence |
| I tablespoon golden syrup | 200 g/7 oz icing sugar, sifted |
| I tablespoon milk | 2 tablespoons chopped nuts |
| 40 g/1½ oz butter | |

1 Make the cake mixture, bake in two prepared 17·5-cm/7-inch sandwich tins as instructions given in One-step Victoria sandwich (see page 79).
2 Place the syrup, milk, butter and coffee essence in a saucepan and heat gently until the butter has melted, stirring occasionally. Add the sifted icing sugar and beat until smooth. Cool until the mixture is thick enough to spread.
3 Sandwich the cakes together with half the icing and use the remainder to cover the top of the cake. Spread smoothly and decorate with a ring of chopped nuts around the edge of the cake.
4 Open freeze before packing.
5 Uncover while frozen and defrost at room temperature.

# No-bake lemon cake

## Makes I cake, 8–10 portions

METRIC/IMPERIAL

| | |
|---|---|
| about 30 boudoir biscuits | 4 eggs, separated |
| 100 g/4 oz butter | finely grated rind and juice of I large lemon |
| 175 g/6 oz castor sugar | |

*when serving:*

| | |
|---|---|
| whipped cream | lemon jelly slices |

1 Line the base and sides of a 20-cm/8-inch cake tin with the boudoir biscuits, placing the sugared sides towards the outside.
2 Cream the butter and sugar together until pale and fluffy. Gradually beat in the egg yolks and the lemon rind and juice. Whisk the egg whites until stiff and fold into the lemon mixture.
3 Spoon part into the lined tin and continue in layers using up the remaining biscuits. Trim the ends of the biscuits around the outside of the tin level with the filling and press the trimmings into the soft lemon mixture.
4 Chill for 12 hours and then open freeze. Turn out of the tin on to a serving plate and return to the freezer until hard before covering.
5 Uncover while still frozen and allow to defrost at room temperature. Serve decorated with whipped cream and lemon jelly slices.

# Coconut fancies

## Makes 12 fancies, 12 portions

METRIC/IMPERIAL

| | |
|---|---|
| I quantity one-step Victoria sandwich mixture (see page 79) | 25 g/1 oz butter |
| 3 tablespoons pineapple juice | 175 g/6 oz icing sugar, sifted |
| finely grated rind of I lemon | 75 g/3 oz desiccated coconut |

1 Make up the cake mixture and spread evenly in a greased and floured 17·5-cm/7-inch by 27·5-cm/11-inch Swiss roll tin.
2 Bake in a moderately hot oven (200°C, 400°F, Gas Mark 6) for about 12 minutes, until firm to the touch. Cool in the tin.
3 Place the pineapple juice, lemon rind and butter in a saucepan and heat gently until the butter has melted. Add the sifted icing sugar and beat until smooth. Cool until the icing begins to thicken.
4 Spread the mixture over the cake, sprinkle with coconut and mark into squares.
5 Open freeze before packing. If preferred, cut the cake into squares before freezing and pack in layers with dividers.
6 Unpack while still frozen and allow to defrost arranged on a plate.

# Coconut gingerbread

## Makes I gingerbread, 9 portions

METRIC/IMPERIAL

| | |
|---|---|
| 175 g/6 oz butter | 75 g/3 oz soft brown sugar |
| 3 tablespoons golden syrup | 75 g/3 oz desiccated coconut |
| 3 tablespoons black treacle | 1½ teaspoons bicarbonate of soda |
| 350 g/12 oz plain flour | 225 ml/7 fl oz warm milk |
| pinch of salt | I egg, beaten |
| 4 teaspoons ground ginger | |

1 Place the butter, golden syrup and black treacle in a saucepan and heat gently until the butter has melted.
2 Sift the flour, salt and ginger into a bowl and stir in the sugar and coconut.
3 Dissolve the bicarbonate of soda in the milk and add to the dry ingredients with the butter mixture and the egg. Beat well until smooth. Pour into a greased and lined 17·5-cm/7-inch square cake tin.
4 Bake in a moderate oven (180°C, 350°F, Gas Mark 4) for about 45 minutes, until well risen. Cool in the tin.
5 Freeze whole or cut into squares before freezing.
6 Defrost at room temperature still sealed in the pack. Cut into squares.

### Variation:

**Spiced sultana gingerbread:** Substitute 75 g/3 oz sultanas for the coconut and add 1 teaspoon mixed spice with the ground ginger.

# Fruity nut cakes

## Makes 24 cakes

METRIC/IMPERIAL

| | |
|---|---|
| 1 quantity one-step Victoria sandwich mixture (see page 79) | 50 g/2 oz sultanas |
| 25 g/1 oz self-raising flour | 25 g/1 oz chopped glacé cherries |
| 50 g/2 oz chopped walnuts | icing sugar |

1 Make up the cake mixture, adding the extra flour. Fold in the nuts and fruit. Divide between 24 paper cake cases standing in bun tins.
2 Bake in a moderately hot oven (190°C, 375°F, Gas Mark 5) for 15–20 minutes, until firm to the touch. Sift the tops lightly with icing sugar.
3 Pack in layers with dividers.
4 Unpack while frozen and arrange on a plate to defrost.

# Chocolate cup cakes

## Makes 24 cup cakes

METRIC/IMPERIAL

| | |
|---|---|
| 1 quantity chocolate almond flavour Victoria sandwich mixture (see page 79) | 2 tablespoons boiling water |
| | 1 tablespoon milk |
| 25 g/1 oz self-raising flour | 75 g/3 oz soft margarine |
| 2 tablespoons cocoa | 225 g/8 oz icing sugar, sifted |

1 Make up the cake mixture, adding the extra flour. Divide between 24 paper cake cases standing in bun tins.
2 Bake in a moderately hot oven (190°C, 375°F, Gas Mark 5) for 15–20 minutes, until firm to the touch.
3 Blend the cocoa with the boiling water until smooth. Add the milk and cool. Cream the margarine with the icing sugar and gradually beat in the cocoa mixture.
4 Spread the tops of the cakes generously with the chocolate mixture.
5 Open freeze before packing in layers with dividers.
6 Unpack while frozen and arrange on a plate to defrost.

# Family sultana cake

## Makes 1 cake, 8–10 portions

METRIC/IMPERIAL

| | |
|---|---|
| 225 g/8 oz self-raising flour | 150 g/5 oz castor sugar |
| 1 teaspoon ground cinnamon | 350 g/12 oz sultanas |
| | 2 eggs, beaten |
| 150 g/5 oz soft margarine | 5 tablespoons milk |
| | 1 tablespoon golden syrup |

1 Sift the flour and spice into a mixing bowl and add all the remaining ingredients. Beat with a wooden spoon for about 3 minutes, until very well blended.
2 Transfer the mixture to a greased and lined 17·5-cm/7-inch cake tin and smooth the top.

3 Bake in a cool oven (150°C, 300°F, Gas Mark 2) for 1¾–2 hours, until a thin skewer inserted in the centre comes out clean. Cool in the tin for 10 minutes then turn out on a wire rack.
4 Pack in a polythene bag before freezing.
5 Defrost at room temperature still sealed in the bag. Sprinkle the top with demerara sugar before serving if wished.

# Almond chocolate gateau

## Makes 1 cake, 6–8 portions

METRIC/IMPERIAL

| | |
|---|---|
| 1 quantity chocolate almond flavour Victoria sandwich mixture (see page 79) | 100 g/4 oz butter |
| | 225 g/8 oz icing sugar, sifted |
| 50 g/2 oz plain chocolate | 50 g/2 oz toasted flaked almonds |

1 Make the cake mixture and turn into a greased and lined 1-kg/2-lb loaf tin. Smooth the top.
2 Bake in a moderate oven (180°C, 350°F, Gas Mark 4) for about 35 minutes, until firm to the touch.
3 Finely grate the chocolate but keep it cold. Cream the butter and icing sugar together until smooth and beat in the grated chocolate.
4 Split the cake into two layers and sandwich together with one third of the filling. Use one further third to cover the sides of the cake and press on the almonds. Spread the remaining filling over the top of the cake and mark with the prongs of a fork into straight lines.
5 Open freeze before packing.
6 Uncover while frozen and allow to defrost at room temperature.

# Chocolate refrigerator cake

## Makes 1 cake, 8–10 portions

METRIC/IMPERIAL

| | |
|---|---|
| 225 g/8 oz plain chocolate | 50 g/2 oz chopped walnuts |
| 450 g/1 lb plain biscuits (e.g. 'Nice') | 2 teaspoons instant coffee |
| 75 g/3 oz castor sugar | 2 tablespoons corn oil |
| 50 g/2 oz glacé cherries, chopped | small can evaporated milk |
| | 2 eggs, beaten |

1 Melt the chocolate in a bowl over a pan of hot water.
2 Crush the biscuits and mix with the sugar, cherries, walnuts and coffee.
3 Gradually stir the oil, evaporated milk and eggs into the melted chocolate. Add this to the dry ingredients and mix well.
4 Transfer to a foil-lined 1-kg/2-lb loaf tin and smooth the top.
5 Open freeze then lift out of the tin and wrap in the foil.
6 Unwrap while frozen, place on a serving dish and allow to defrost at room temperature.

# Whisked mocha gateau

## Makes 1 cake, 6–8 portions

METRIC/IMPERIAL

4 eggs
1 tablespoon coffee essence
100 g/4 oz castor sugar

75 g/3 oz plain flour
1 tablespoon cornflour
1 tablespoon cocoa

*decoration:*

75 g/3 oz butter
175 g/6 oz icing sugar, sifted
2 tablespoons coffee essence

2 tablespoons Tia Maria or Kahlua (optional)

*when serving:*

1 chocolate 'flake'

1 Place the eggs in a bowl with the coffee essence and sugar and whisk with an electric mixer until pale and thick and doubled in bulk. If whisking by hand place the bowl over a pan of simmering water. When thick, remove from the heat and whisk until cold.
2 Sift the flour with the cornflour and cocoa and fold into the whisked mixture. Divide between two greased and base-lined 20-cm/8-inch sandwich tins.
3 Bake in a moderately hot oven (190°C, 375°F, Gas Mark 5) for about 20 minutes, until golden brown and firm to the touch. Cool on a wire rack.
4 Cream the butter with the icing sugar until smooth and gradually beat in the coffee essence. Sprinkle the liqueur over the cake layers.
5 Use half the filling mixture to sandwich the layers together and spread the remaining mixture over the top of the cake.
6 Place on a serving plate or board and open freeze before wrapping.
7 Unwrap while still frozen and allow to defrost at room temperature. Crumble the 'flake' and press the pieces into the top of the cake like 'spikes'.

# Shortbread fingers

## Makes 24 fingers

METRIC/IMPERIAL

225 g/8 oz butter
100 g/4 oz castor sugar

225 g/8 oz plain flour
100 g/4 oz cornflour

1 Cream the butter and sugar together until pale and fluffy.
2 Sift the flour and cornflour together and gradually work into the creamed mixture. Knead until smooth.
3 Press into a shallow tin about 30 cm/12 inches by 20 cm/8 inches. Prick all over with a fork and bake in a moderate oven (160°C, 325°F, Gas Mark 3) for 30–40 minutes.
4 Cut into fingers (7·5 cm/3 inches by 2·5 cm/1 inch while still hot. Cool in the tin and sprinkle with castor sugar.
5 Pack in layers with dividers.
6 Unpack and arrange on a plate to defrost.

# Mincemeat shortbread sandwich

## Makes 6 portions

METRIC/IMPERIAL

½ basic quantity shortbread mix (see this page)

350 g/12 oz mincemeat
2 tablespoons demerara sugar

1 Make up the shortbread mix and place half in the base of a greased 20-cm/8-inch foil flan case. Cover with the mincemeat.
2 Knead the sugar into the remaining shortbread mix and spread this carefully over the mincemeat to cover it completely. Mark the top decoratively with a fork.
3 Bake in a cool oven (150°C, 300°F, Gas Mark 2) for about 50 minutes, or until the top is golden brown.
4 Cool and freeze in the foil case.
5 Defrost and cut into wedges with a sharp knife.

# Basic chilled cheesecake

## Makes 6 portions

METRIC/IMPERIAL

1 tablespoon gelatine
2 tablespoons water
225 g/8 oz cottage cheese, sieved
225 g/8 oz cream cheese
25 g/1 oz icing sugar
2 eggs, separated

150 ml/¼ pint single cream
finely grated rind and juice of ½ lemon
100 g/4 oz butter
225 g/8 oz digestive biscuits

1 Dissolve the gelatine in the water in a basin over a pan of hot water. Cool.
2 Beat the cottage cheese, cream cheese and sugar until well blended. Add the egg yolks and cream and beat until smooth. Stir in the dissolved gelatine and the lemon rind and juice. When the mixture thickens, stiffly whisk the egg whites and fold in lightly.
3 Pour the mixture into a 20-cm/8-inch loose-bottomed cake tin. Freeze until firm.
4 Melt the butter, stir in the biscuit crumbs and sprinkle this mixture over the top of the cheesecake. Press with the back of a tablespoon to make a smooth firm crust. Return to the freezer until hard.
5 Dip the tin in warm water and turn the cheesecake on to a plate. Lift off the base of the tin and allow the cheesecake to harden in the freezer again before wrapping.
6 When required to serve, uncover while still frozen and allow to defrost at room temperature.

## Variations:

**Cherry-topped cheesecake:** When the cheesecake has defrosted, carefully spread a 396-g/14-oz can of cherry pie filling over the top.

**Curd cheesecake:** Use 450 g/1 lb curd cheese instead of the cottage and cream cheeses. Add extra sugar if necessary.

**Soured cream cheesecake:** Substitute 150 ml/¼ pint soured cream for the single cream and add 1 extra tablespoon of lemon juice.

**Rich orange cheesecake:** Use 450 g/1 lb cream cheese instead of half cottage and half cream cheese, 150 ml/¼ pint double cream instead of the single cream and the finely grated rind and juice of 1 large orange instead of the lemon rind and juice.

**Lemon chocolate cheesecake:** Use the finely grated rind of 1 whole lemon and extra 1 tablespoon of juice in the filling. Crush 225 g/8 oz chocolate digestive biscuits and use in place of the plain digestive biscuits. When the cheesecake has defrosted, grate a little chocolate over the top.

## Pineapple cheese pie

### Makes 6 portions
METRIC/IMPERIAL

| | |
|---|---|
| 175 g/6 oz shortcrust pastry (see page 67) | I egg, beaten |
| 225 g/8 oz cottage cheese | 6 tablespoons milk |
| 75 g/3 oz castor sugar | 50 g/2 oz flour |
| 25 g/I oz butter, melted | 367-g/13-oz can crushed pineapple, drained |

1 Roll out the pastry and use to line a 20-cm/8-inch sandwich tin. Bake 'blind' in a moderately hot oven (200°C, 400°F, Gas Mark 6) for 15 minutes. Remove the paper and baking beans and return to the oven for a further 5 minutes. Cool. Reduce oven heat to moderate (180°C, 350°F, Gas Mark 4).
2 Meanwhile, sieve the cottage cheese and beat in the sugar, melted butter, egg and milk. Sift the flour and stir thoroughly into the cheese mixture with the pineapple.
3 Turn into the pastry case and smooth the top. Bake for about 20 minutes, until the filling is set and the top pale golden. Cool.
4 Open freeze then remove from the tin before packing.
5 Unwrap, place on a serving dish and defrost at room temperature.

# Biscuits and cookies

## Peanut cookies

### Makes about 60 cookies
METRIC/IMPERIAL

| | |
|---|---|
| 225 g/8 oz butter | 450 g/I lb self-raising flour |
| 100 g/4 oz peanut butter | |
| 450 g/I lb castor sugar | 100 g/4 oz salted peanuts, chopped |
| 2 eggs, beaten | |

1 Cream the butter, peanut butter and sugar together and gradually beat in the egg. Fold in the flour and peanuts, form into a dough and knead lightly.
2 Divide into two equal portions and shape each into a roll about 5 cm/2 inches in diameter.
3 Wrap the rolls in foil and freeze before cooking.
4 Unwrap and cut thin slices from the frozen roll with a sharp knife. Arrange on greased baking sheets and bake in a moderately hot oven (190°C, 375°F, Gas Mark 5) for about 10 minutes, until pale golden. Cool on a wire rack.

### Variations:

**Apricot cookies:** Substitute an extra 100 g/4 oz butter and omit the peanut butter. Substitute 100 g/4 oz finely chopped dried apricots for the peanuts.

**Chocolate cookies:** Substitute an extra 100 g/4 oz butter for the peanut butter, 40 g/1½ oz cocoa for 40 g/1½ oz of the flour and use 100 g/4 oz coarsely grated plain chocolate instead of the peanuts.

**Cinnamon date cookies:** Substitute an extra 100 g/4 oz butter for the peanut butter and add 4 teaspoons ground cinnamon with the flour. Use 100 g/4 oz chopped dates instead of the peanuts.

## Almond honey fingers

### Makes about 60 fingers
METRIC/IMPERIAL

| | |
|---|---|
| 150 g/5 oz butter | 225 g/8 oz plain flour |
| 4 tablespoons clear honey | pinch of salt |
| I egg, beaten | 350 g/12 oz ground almonds |
| I teaspoon almond essence | |

1 Cream the butter and honey and gradually beat in the egg and almond essence. Add the flour, salt and almonds and mix until smooth.
2 Place some of the mixture in a piping bag fitted with a star nozzle. Pipe the mixture in fingers on greased baking sheets and bake in a hot oven (220°C, 425°F, Gas Mark 7) for about 8 minutes, or until pale golden. Cool on a wire rack. Repeat with the remaining dough.
3 Freeze in rigid-based containers for protection.
4 Unpack and arrange on a serving dish to defrost.

**Variation:**

**Almond kisses:** Pipe the mixture in rosettes, freeze and when defrosted, sandwich together in pairs with vanilla butter cream made by beating 50 g/2 oz butter with 100 g/4 oz sifted icing sugar and ½ teaspoon vanilla essence until smooth. Sift tops with icing sugar.

## Hazlenut crisps

### Makes about 50 biscuits

METRIC/IMPERIAL

| | |
|---|---|
| 350 g/12 oz self-raising flour | 2 teaspoons vanilla essence |
| 350 g/12 oz castor sugar | 225 g/8 oz chopped toasted hazelnuts |
| 225 g/8 oz butter | |
| 2 eggs, beaten | 1 egg white |

1 Mix together the flour and sugar and rub in the butter. Add the beaten egg, vanilla and nuts and mix thoroughly.
2 Divide the mixture into balls the size of a walnut and place well apart on baking sheets. Whisk the egg white lightly, use to brush the biscuits and bake in a hot oven (220°C, 425°F, Gas Mark 7) for about 10 minutes.
3 Pack in rigid-based containers for protection.
4 Unpack and allow to defrost on a serving dish.

**Variations:**

**Walnut crisps:** Substitute 225 g/8 oz chopped walnuts for the hazelnuts and use 2 teaspoons coffee essence instead of the vanilla.

**Coconut crisps:** Substitute 225 g/8 oz desiccated coconut for the hazelnuts and use 2 teaspoons milk instead of the vanilla essence.

# Cold desserts

## Apple mallow mousse

### Makes 4 portions

METRIC/IMPERIAL

| | |
|---|---|
| 2 teaspoons gelatine | few drops green food colouring |
| 2 tablespoons water | 2 egg whites |
| 150-g/5-oz packet marshmallows | |
| 300 ml/½ pint apple purée | |

1 Dissolve the gelatine in the water in a basin over a pan of hot water. Cool.
2 Place the marshmallows in a bowl and melt over the pan of hot water. Stir in the apple purée, dissolved gelatine and green food colouring.
3 When the mixture is on the point of setting, whisk the egg whites until stiff and fold in lightly.
4 Spoon into 4 glasses or individual polythene containers and allow to set.
5 Cover with cling wrap or foil and smooth down the edges, or snap on the seals before freezing.
6 Uncover and allow to defrost at room temperature.

**Variation:**

**Marbled mallow mousse:** Use the same quantities as above but make up into two separate basins, using the pink marshmallows for one and the white marshmallows for the other. Tint the mixtures pink and green and spoon them alternately into the containers, or into one larger dish.

## Apricot cream mousse

### Makes 8 portions

METRIC/IMPERIAL

| | |
|---|---|
| 1 tablespoon gelatine | 300 ml/½ pint double cream |
| 2 tablespoons water | 2 egg whites |
| sugar | |
| 300 ml/½ pint apricot purée | |

1 Dissolve the gelatine in the water in a basin over hot water. Cool.
2 Sweeten the fruit purée to taste and stir in the dissolved gelatine.
3 When the mixture begins to thicken, whip the cream until thick and fold in. Whisk the egg whites until stiff, fold in lightly until the mixture is well blended and no streaks of egg white are visible.
4 Spoon into 8 individual containers, or 1 large dish and allow to set.
5 Cover containers with foil or cling wrap and smooth down the edges before freezing.
6 Uncover while frozen and allow to defrost at room temperature.

## Variations:

**Prune cream mousse:** Drain, stone and purée a 425-g/15-oz can of prunes and add sufficient syrup from the can to make the purée up to 300 ml/½ pint. Use this instead of the apricot purée.

**Raspberry cream mousse:** Substitute 300 ml/½ pint sieved raspberries for the apricot purée.

**Apple and raspberry cream mousse:** Substitute 150 ml/¼ pint apple purée and 150 ml/¼ pint sieved raspberries for the apricot purée.

# Chocolate ratafia mould

### Makes 4–6 portions

METRIC/IMPERIAL

| | |
|---|---|
| 450 ml/¾ pint milk | 150 ml/¼ pint double |
| 35 g/1¼ oz cocoa | cream |
| 1 tablespoon gelatine | 75 g/3 oz ratafias or |
| 100 g/4 oz sugar | macaroons, crushed |
| ½ teaspoon almond essence | |

1 Place the milk in a saucepan and gradually whisk in the cocoa. Bring to boiling point and remove from the heat. Sprinkle in the gelatine and whisk until it has completely dissolved. Add the sugar and almond essence, stir well and allow to cool.
2 When the mixture is on the point of setting, whip the cream until thick, stir in the ratafias and fold this into the chocolate mixture.
3 Turn into a lightly oiled mould and allow to set.
4 Cover mould with foil or cling wrap and smooth down the edges before freezing.
5 Uncover, allow to defrost in the refrigerator then turn out on a serving dish. Decorate with whipped cream if wished.

### Variation:

**Mocha macaroon mould:** Substitute 2 teaspoons instant coffee for the almond essence.

# Coffee cheesecake mousse

### Makes 4–6 portions

METRIC/IMPERIAL

| | |
|---|---|
| 1 tablespoon gelatine | 2 tablespoons coffee |
| 3 tablespoons water | essence |
| 225 g/8 oz cream cheese | 2 egg whites |
| 1 large can condensed milk | |

1 Dissolve the gelatine in the water in a basin over hot water. Cool.
2 Beat the cream cheese until smooth and gradually add the condensed milk and coffee essence. Stir in the dissolved gelatine.
3 When the mixture is on the point of setting, whisk the egg whites until stiff and fold in lightly.
4 Pour into a glass dish and allow to set.

5 Cover dish with foil or cling wrap and smooth down the edges before freezing.
6 Uncover and allow to defrost at room temperature. If liked, scatter 1 tablespoon toasted flaked almonds over the top before serving.

### Variations:

**Orange cheesecake mousse:** Substitute 2 tablespoons orange juice and the finely grated rind of 4 large orange for the coffee essence.

**Caramel cheesecake mousse:** Heat 2 tablespoons granulated sugar and 1 tablespoon water in a small saucepan without stirring until golden brown. Remove from the heat, add 2 tablespoons cold water and stir until dissolved. Add to the mixture in place of the coffee essence. Use 2 tablespoons water only to dissolve the gelatine.

**Rum and chocolate cheesecake mousse:** Melt 50 g/2 oz plain chocolate in a basin over a pan of hot water and stir into the mixture with 1 tablespoon rum. Omit the coffee essence.

# Marbled cherry trifles

### Makes 4 portions

METRIC/IMPERIAL

| | |
|---|---|
| 2 trifle sponges | 300 ml/½ pint canned |
| 2 tablespoons sweet sherry | ready-to-serve custard |
| 150 ml/¼ pint canned cherry pie filling | 150 ml/¼ pint double cream |

1 Crumble the sponges and place in the bases of 4 deep sundae glasses or polythene parfait dishes. Moisten the sponge with the sherry.
2 Stir the pie filling into the custard and divide among the containers. Whip the cream and pipe small rosettes over the tops of the trifles but try to keep the top of the decoration below the rim of the containers to avoid damage.
3 Open freeze before covering or snapping on the seals.
4 Uncover while still frozen and allow to defrost at room temperature.

### Variations:

**Mandarin custard trifles:** Substitute 100 g/4 oz drained canned mandarins for the pie filling and use 2 tablespoons Grand Marnier or Orange Curaçao instead of the sherry. Arrange the oranges on the sponge and spoon the custard over the top.

**Banana custard trifles:** Substitute 1 large sliced banana and 2 tablespoons lemon curd for the pie filling and use 2 tablespoons orange or pineapple juice instead of the sherry. Mix the banana and lemon curd and use to top the sponge before spooning in the custard.

## Crunchy orange sandwich

**Makes 4–6 portions**

METRIC/IMPERIAL
75 g/3 oz butter
175 g/6 oz digestive
  biscuits, crushed
1 tablespoon cornflour
150 ml/¼ pint water
175 g/6 oz sugar
2 eggs, separated

3 teaspoons finely grated
  orange rind
¼ teaspoon salt
4 tablespoons orange
  juice
300 ml/½ pint double
  cream

1 Melt the butter, stir in the biscuit crumbs and use half this mixture to cover the base of a 20-cm/8-inch cake tin with a loose base. Press flat with the back of a metal spoon and chill.
2 Moisten the cornflour with a little of the water and place in a small saucepan with the remaining water and the sugar. Stir over heat until the mixture comes to the boil and is clear and thick. Remove from the heat, beat in the egg yolks, orange rind and salt. Place over a larger saucepan of boiling water and stir until the egg yolks thicken the mixture slightly. Do not overcook. Remove from the heat, beat in the orange juice and chill. Whip the cream until thick, whisk the egg whites until stiff, and fold these into the orange mixture. Pour over the chilled biscuit base and sprinkle with the remaining crumb mixture.
3 Open freeze until solid then remove from the tin, slide off the base of the tin on to a plate or board and cover with foil or cling wrap.
4 Uncover and allow to defrost in the refrigerator for 2 hours. Serve while still semi-frozen.

**Variations:**

**Crunchy pineapple sandwich:** Substitute 100 g/4 oz drained canned crushed pineapple for the orange rind and juice. Stir in before the mixture is chilled.

**Crunchy lemon sandwich:** Substitute 2 teaspoons finely grated lemon rind for the orange rind and 4 tablespoons lemon juice for the orange juice.

## Ice cream flan

**Makes 4–6 portions**

METRIC/IMPERIAL
40 g/1½ oz butter
3 tablespoons golden
  syrup
75 g/3 oz corn flakes

100 g/4 oz grapes
25 g/1 oz flaked almonds
600 ml/1 pint vanilla ice
  cream

1 Melt the butter with the golden syrup and stir in the corn flakes. Press this mixture to the base and sides of a 20-cm/8-inch foil flan case. Chill.
2 Halve and pip the grapes and arrange in the corn flake case with the nuts. Cover with slightly over-lapping scoops of ice cream.
3 Open freeze until solid before covering.
4 Uncover while frozen and allow to defrost in the refrigerator for 20 minutes before serving.

**Variations:**

**Krispie ice cream flan:** Substitute 50 g/2 oz rice Krispies for the 75 g/3 oz corn flakes.

**Chocolate ice cream flan:** Add 1 tablespoon drinking chocolate to the butter and syrup mixture and use 600 ml/1 pint chocolate ice cream instead of vanilla ice cream.

**Jelly mousse flan:** Substitute a filling made by dissolving a 600-ml/1-pint packet of any fruit jelly in 150 ml/¼ pint boiling water. Cool until beginning to set. Whisk 200 ml/7 fl oz evaporated milk until thick and gradually whisk in the setting jelly. Pour into the flan case before freezing. Defrost fully and serve at room temperature.

# Uncooked freezer jam

## All-fruit berry jam

**Makes about 2·75 kg/6 lb jam**

METRIC/IMPERIAL
1 kg/2 lb raspberries,
  loganberries,
  strawberries,
  blackberries,
  blackcurrants or
  redcurrants

4 tablespoons lemon juice
1·5 kg/3½ lb castor sugar
225-g/8-oz bottle fruit
  pectin

1 Place the fruit in a bowl with the lemon juice and sugar and stir well. Crush the fruit lightly with a wooden spoon to start the juice flowing. Allow the mixture to stand at room temperature until the sugar has completely dissolved, stirring occasionally. This may take up to 48 hours. Stir in the pectin and leave to stand until the jam begins to thicken.
2 Divide between polythene or glass containers and seal. Keep the jam at room temperature for a further 12 hours before freezing.
3 Defrost in the sealed pack for about 30 minutes before serving. Store opened containers in the refrigerator.

# Ice creams and sorbets

## Basic vanilla ice cream

### Makes 8 portions

METRIC/IMPERIAL
I large can evaporated milk, chilled
2 eggs, separated
100 g/4 oz castor sugar
I teaspoon vanilla essence

1 Whip the evaporated milk until really thick. In another bowl, whisk the egg yolks, sugar and vanilla essence together until pale and thick and the sugar has completely dissolved. Fold the mixtures together. Stiffly whisk the egg whites, and fold in lightly.
2 Divide between shallow containers and freeze until firm.
3 Defrost in the refrigerator for 20 minutes before scooping.

### Variations:

**Coffee ice cream:** Add 2 tablespoons coffee essence to the egg yolk mixture in place of the vanilla essence.

**Lemon ice cream:** Omit the vanilla essence and whip the milk with 5 tablespoons lemon juice and the finely grated rind of 1 lemon.

## Simple baked Alaska

### Makes 6–8 portions

METRIC/IMPERIAL
2 tablespoons red jam
I baked 20-cm/8-inch sponge flan case
100 g/4 oz drained canned peaches
600 ml/I pint vanilla ice cream
2 egg whites
pinch of cream of tartar
100 g/4 oz castor sugar

1 Spread the jam in the flan case and arrange the peaches on top. Pile up the ice cream in the centre, leaving a border of sponge 2·5 cm/1 inch wide all round. Open freeze until firm.
2 Whisk the egg whites until stiff, add the cream of tartar and 2 tablespoons sugar and continue whisking until thick and glossy. Fold in the remaining sugar.
3 Swirl the meringue all over the ice cream, sealing it well to the border of sponge round the outside. Open freeze before covering lightly with cling wrap.
4 Uncover and place immediately in a hot oven (230°C, 450°F, Gas Mark 8) for 4–5 minutes, until golden brown. Serve at once.

### Variation:

**Chocolate mint Alaska:** Substitute 600 ml/1 pint chocolate mint ice cream and use 1 large sliced banana in place of the peaches.

## Cherry crumb bombe

### Makes 4–6 portions

METRIC/IMPERIAL
75 g/3 oz butter
175 g/6 oz digestive biscuits, crushed
I tablespoon sugar
150 ml/¼ pint double cream
2 tablespoons rum
396-g/14-oz can cherry pie filling

1 Melt the butter, stir in the biscuit crumbs and sugar and tip into a 1-litre/1¾-pint pudding basin. Press a smaller pudding basin into the crumbs until there is an even layer over the base and sides of the larger pudding basin. Chill until firm and remove the smaller basin.
2 Whip the cream until just thick. Stir in the rum and the pie filling to give a marbled effect. Spoon this into the biscuit crumb crust and smooth the top.
3 Freeze in the pudding basin.
4 Dip basin in hot water and turn bombe out on a serving dish. Defrost in the refrigerator for 45 minutes. The centre should be softened but still frozen.

### Variation:

**Strawberry crumb bombe:** Substitute a 396-g/14-oz can of strawberry pie filling for the cherry pie filling and use 2 tablespoons sweet sherry instead of the rum.

## Blackberry sorbet

### Makes 4–6 portions

METRIC/IMPERIAL
450 g/I lb blackberries
300 ml/½ pint water
sugar
I teaspoon gelatine
2 egg whites

1 Place the blackberries in a saucepan with the water and simmer until tender. Add sugar to taste and the gelatine and stir until the gelatine has completely dissolved.
2 Sieve to obtain a smooth purée. Alternatively, liquidise and then sieve the purée. Pour into a shallow container and freeze until mushy.
3 Whisk the egg whites until stiff, turn the blackberry mixture into a bowl, beat until smooth and fold in the egg whites.
4 Return to the freezer until firm.
5 Uncover and defrost at room temperature for 10 minutes before scooping.

### Variations:

**Apricot sorbet:** Substitute 450 g/1 lb stoned ripe apricots for the blackberries. Liquidise the cooked fruit mixture until smooth. There is no need to sieve.

**Raspberry sorbet:** Substitute 450 g/1 lb raspberries for the blackberries and sieve without cooking. Dissolve the gelatine in the water in a saucepan and add to the raspberry purée with sugar to taste.

# Index